If Not for the Grace of God

Learning To Live
Independently From
Struggles and Frustrations

If Not for the Grace of God

Learning To Live
Independently From
Struggles and Frustrations

by

Joyce Meyer

Harrison House
Tulsa, Oklahoma

16th Printing

If Not for the Grace of God:
Learning to Live Independent of Frustrations and Struggles
ISBN 0-89274-796-X
Copyright © 1995 by Joyce Meyer
Life In The Word, Inc.
P. O. Box 655
Fenton, Missouri 63026

Published by Harrison House, Inc.
P. O. Box 35035
Tulsa, Oklahoma 74153

Contents

Introduction

In these pages I am going to be sharing with you some dynamic statements about grace. Grace is the power of God available to meet our needs without any cost to us. It is received by believing rather than through human effort.

I sincerely believe that if you will take these statements and meditate upon them, they will literally change your walk with the Lord.

In the past several years we have heard a lot of teaching about faith: what faith is, what it is not, and how to operate in it. In spite of all that, to be very honest with you, I am not sure how many believers truly understand faith. If we really understood as much about faith as we claim, we would be seeing much more victory in our daily lives than what we see.

All knowledge of faith must be built upon a clear understanding of grace. One of the things I will be sharing with you in these pages is a prophecy, a word that I received from the Lord in which He defines grace and describes its role and function in the life of the believer.

Actually the grace of God is not complicated or confusing. It is simple, and that's why many people miss it. There is nothing more powerful than grace. In fact, everything in the Bible — salvation, the infilling of the Holy Spirit, fellowship with God and all victory in our daily lives — is based upon it. Without grace, we are nothing, we have nothing, we can do nothing. If it were not for the grace of God, we would all be miserable and hopeless.

In Luke 2:40 we are told that as a child, Jesus **...grew and became strong in spirit, filled with wisdom; and the grace (favor and spiritual blessing) of God was upon Him**.

This verse contains everything we need to be happy, healthy, prosperous and successful in our Christian walk. We often talk about all the things we need, but in reality there is only one thing that we need, and it is the same thing that Jesus needed: we need to become strong in spirit, filled with God's wisdom and having His grace upon us.

If you and I will allow the grace of God to have full reign in our life, nothing will be impossible to us. Without that grace, nothing is possible to us.

As Paul wrote to the believers in his day, everything we are and do and have is by the grace of God. You and I are one hundred percent helpless. Although we often confess as Paul did, "I can do all things through Christ Who strengthens me," that is only true by the grace of God.

In Ephesians 2:10 Paul tells us that **...we are God's [own] handiwork (His workmanship), recreated in Christ Jesus, [born anew] that we may do those good works which God predestined (planned beforehand) for us [taking paths which He prepared ahead of time], that we should walk in them [living the good life which He prearranged and made ready for us to live]**. The writer of Hebrews tells us our works were prepared for us by God **...from the foundation of the world** (Heb. 4:3). According to these verses, God chose us and laid out our life work for us before we were ever born, before the world was even created. That's why we must stop talking about "our" ministry, as though it is something that we undertake on our own initiative or carry out by our own ability. In John 15:5 Jesus said, **...apart from Me [cut off from vital union with Me] you can do nothing**.

Instead of boasting of our great strength or knowledge or power or accomplishments, we should begin each day by saying, "Here am I, Lord, ready for whatever You have for me to do. I empty myself, as much as I know how, to allow Your grace to flow in my life, to cause me to be able to do whatever it is that You desire for me. I cast myself totally upon You. I can be only what You allow me to be, I can have only what You will for me to have, I can do only what You empower me to do — and each victory is to Your glory, not mine."

You and I are the vessels through which God does His own works. We are partners with God. What an awesome privilege! He allows us to share in His glory as long as we remember that apart from Him we can do nothing.

If we really believe that God is in complete control of our life, none of the things that go wrong will upset or discourage us, because we will know that through it all God is working out *His* plan for us. We will not glory in what *we* are doing for God, but only in what *He* is doing through us.

We must learn to commit our lives to God, trusting ourselves to Him in everything and for everything, relying not upon our great faith but upon His marvelous grace. It is true that faith is important, but even faith comes to us by grace, as a gift. Everything in our lives depends, not upon our merits or abilities or works, but upon God's divine willingness to use His infinite power to meet our needs — and at no cost to us whatsoever.

That is grace.

If you have needs today — and who doesn't? — I urge you to cast them upon the Lord. It is fine to have plans and goals and dreams for your life; it is wonderful to have things that you are believing God for, but I suggest that you make a commitment to put all that aside for a moment. Just for the time it takes to read this book, free yourself from all attempts to *achieve* anything by your own faith and effort. Instead, just relax and place your trust solely upon the Lord. Let go completely and see what dynamic power He will bring to bear in Your life as you simply yield yourself to *receive* His amazing grace. I believe you will see such a change in your entire approach to life that you will never desire to return to old ways.

1
Grace, Grace and More Grace

1

Grace, Grace and More Grace

As we begin our study of the grace of God, I would like to share with you briefly about the condition that my life was in when the Lord first began to give me a revelation about what grace actually is.

At that time I had little revelation about the subject, but as I studied, I was really stirred up in my spirit to believe God for a greater revelation. As you read, I want to encourage you to be in faith asking God to give you a deeper revelation about this wonderful thing called grace.

The Word Is Frustrating

When God first began to reveal to me what grace actually is, I suppose I was about as frustrated as anybody can be. Why was I so frustrated? There were many different reasons for my frustration, but one of the things that was frustrating me the most was, believe it or not, the Word of God.

How could the Word be frustrating me? The reason is simple. As is so often the case with believers, I was trying to *work the Word* rather than *letting the Word work in me*. The thing that was frustrating me about the Word was this: it kept convicting me.

You see, I had a lot of problems in my life, but I didn't really know the source of my problems. I thought they were being caused by somebody else. I was convinced that if everyone else would change and act differently, then I could finally be happy and content. Then when I started studying the Word of God, it began to reveal to me that there were lots of areas in my life that needed to be changed. Every message I heard, whether it was on television, or on radio, on cassette or in a meeting, seemed to convict me of my need to be changed. The problem was that I didn't understand the difference between conviction and condemnation.

As the Word would bring me to conviction, which is what it is designed by the Lord to do, the devil would take that thing that was intended for my good and would begin to beat me over the head with it as condemnation. I would look in the Word and see my need to change, but I didn't know anything about the grace of God to bring about that change in me. I didn't know how to allow the Spirit of the Lord to come into my life and cause the things to happen that needed to happen as I believed Him and exercised my faith. I thought *I* had to do it all.

I was trying to change myself, trying to make myself be everything that the Word said that I was supposed to be. I didn't know how to submit myself to the Lord and wait on Him. I knew nothing about being changed from glory to glory (2 Cor. 3:18 KJV), about conquering my enemies little by little. (Deut. 7:22.)

Besides trying to change myself, I was also trying to change everything else in my life. I was trying to change my husband, my children, all my circumstances, everything that I thought was the root cause of my problems. I tried and tried and tried until I felt I would die from frustration. *Trying to do something about something you can't do anything about is frustrating!*

What I was doing was operating under the Law, which the Bible says will always lead to frustration and, eventually, to disappointment and destruction.

The Law Versus Grace

And all who depend on the Law [who are seeking to be justified by obedience to the Law of rituals] are under a curse and doomed to disappointment and destruction, for it is written in the Scriptures, Cursed (accursed, devoted to destruction, doomed to eternal punishment) be everyone who does not continue to abide (live and remain) by all the precepts and commands written in the Book of the Law and to practice them.

Galatians 3:10

I didn't realize my problem was that by all my trying I was unconsciously putting myself under the curse of the Law. I was taking this good thing of the Word of God and making a law out of it. I saw all of it as something I had to accomplish rather than promises God would fulfill in me as I trusted Him and waited for His victory. Do you know that you and I can make a law out of every word in the Bible if we don't know how to approach it properly?

Any time we put ourselves under the Law, we are setting ourselves up for misery. Why? Because the Law has the ability to do one of two things: If we follow it perfectly, it can make us holy. But since no human being can do that, the second thing the Law can do is to actually increase sin, which leads to destruction.

Romans 2 and 3 teach us that God gave the Old Testament Law so man would try to keep it, find out he could not, and realize his desperate need for a savior.

How does that happen? We hear or read the Law and conclude, "If I don't follow this Law, I am going to lose my salvation" or "God won't love me if I don't behave properly. He won't love me if I am not good." We then begin to look at the Word totally opposite from the way God wants us to see it. All He wants us to do is to face the truth and say, "Yes, Lord, You're absolutely right. I need to do that. I need to change, but I can't change myself. Your Word is truth, and my life is not matching up to it. Your Word has become a mirror to me. In it I can see that I am wrong in this area, and I am sorry. I ask You to forgive me and to change me by Your power and Your grace."

But I didn't know how to do that. I didn't know anything about the power of God and the grace of God. All I knew about was trying — trying to be good, trying to do everything that the Word said that I should do. Trying not to talk too much, trying to submit, trying to be more generous, trying to operate in the fruit of the Spirit. Trying to pray more, trying to read the Bible more, trying to understand the Bible more when I did read it. Trying to be a better wife, trying to be a better mother — on and on.

As a result, I was totally frustrated.

One meaning of the word *frustrate* is to disappoint, to prevent from obtaining a goal or fulfilling a desire.[1]

As Paul describes so well in Galatians 3:10, I was frustrated — disappointed and actually being destroyed — because I was trying to live by a Law that was totally impossible for me to keep. I was trying to obtain a goal and fulfill a desire that was beyond my ability. The harder I tried, the more miserably I failed.

When you and I put all our energy and effort into something that is doomed to failure, the only possible result is frustration. And all we know to do about the situation is to try harder — which only produces more frustration.

It is a vicious cycle, one that can be broken only by a proper understanding of the grace of God.

---

[1]Based on definition *Webster's New World Dictionary,* 3rd college ed., s.v. "frustrate."

Trying Versus Trusting

Do you realize that the word *try* is unscriptural? I know that is true because I checked in the largest concordance I could find. Oh, the word is there all right, but not in the sense that we are using it in this context.

The only way *try* is used in the Bible is in the sense of putting someone or something to the test. The Bible speaks of the "trying of our faith." (James 1:3 KJV.) We are told not to believe everything that we hear, but to "try the spirits." (1 John 4:1 KJV.) The psalmist says, "Try me, O Lord, and know my thoughts." (Ps. 139:23 KJV.) The Bible also talks about fiery trials which will "try" us. (1 Pet. 4:12 KJV.) In the scriptural sense, then, the word *try* refers to a test or trial to determine the value and worth of a person or thing.

But that is totally different from the way we usually use the word *try* — which is in referring to human effort. We say we are "trying" when we are attempting to achieve or accomplish something by our own means or ability.

Now I am not saying that we should never make any effort to achieve or accomplish anything in life. Not at all. One of the messages I often preach is on the subject of the proper effort we are to put out as believers, an effort that is made through the power and by the grace of God at work within us. In other words, we don't attempt anything without asking for God's help. We lean on Him the whole way through each project. We maintain an attitude that says, "Apart from Him I can do nothing."

But we are not to be involved in natural, carnal efforts because the result is only fatigue and frustration, disappointment and destruction.

As you read these pages, I would like to suggest that you be willing to exchange trying for trusting. That's what I learned to do as the Lord opened to me a whole new realm of revelation about His marvelous grace.

The Source of Strife

What leads to strife (discord and feuds) and how do conflicts (quarrels and fightings) originate among you? Do they not arise from your sensual desires that are ever warring in your bodily members?

James 4:1

Do you have strife, discord, feuds, conflicts and wars going on within your own self? There was a time when my life was literally filled with strife.

How does all this disturbance get started within us? We know that it is not God's will for us. The Lord does not want His children to live in the midst of a constant interior war zone. That is the nature of this world in which we live, but it is not supposed to be the nature of the Kingdom of God — and Jesus has told us that the Kingdom is within us. (Luke 17:21.)

One reason you and I came to Christ in the first place is because we wanted to escape all that kind of endless strife and conflict. That is why we became citizens of the Kingdom of God. The Bible tells us that the Kingdom is righteousness, peace and joy. (Rom. 14:17 KJV.) As followers of Jesus Christ, that is our heritage and our inheritance. Why is it, then, that so many of us who truly love God, who are going to heaven, who are the called according to His divine purpose, still spend our whole earthly existence in the midst of what we are trying so desperately to escape from?

What is the source of all this strife? Where does it originate? That is the question that we want to answer in order to discover the solution to our frustration and misery.

But notice the second part of this verse. James tells us that all these negative things arise from the sensual desires that are ever warring in our members.

Do you know that you and I can get into conflict by wanting something that is clearly God's will for us? Having God's will in our lives can frustrate us. If we go about trying to get it in the wrong way, we will only produce strife and war and conflict.

God wants our spouse and our children to be saved. We know that is His will because He has said in His Word that He desires that all people come to a saving knowledge of Him. (2 Pet. 3:9.) Yet you and I can get frustrated — and cause all kinds of misery for ourselves and others — if we go about trying to get our loved ones saved by our own human efforts.

As strange as it may sound, it is entirely possible to get into war over the Word of God. It happens all the time within the Body of Christ.

It is certainly God's will for us to live holy lives, but I can't tell you how much conflict I caused in my life trying to be holy. I wanted all the right things, but I went about getting them in all the wrong ways. That is what James is warning us about here in this verse. He is saying that strife and conflict arise within us because our desires — even possibly our righteous desires — are warring in our bodily members.

We Have Not Because We Ask Not

You are jealous and covet [what others have] and your desires go unfulfilled; [so] you become murderers. [To hate is to murder as far as your hearts are concerned.] You burn with envy and anger and are not able to obtain [the gratification, the contentment, and the happiness that you seek], so you fight and war. You do not have, because you do not ask.

James 4:2

People in church get into wars over prophetic gifts and musical gifts. They become jealous of each other because one sings and another doesn't. They hate one another simply because they do not have something the other person has. Jealousy and envy are not love. God refers to them as hatred.

The Bible gets pretty strenuous about this point. It says that to hate others because of their special gifts is to become a murderer in the heart.

Are you and I guilty of murder in our hearts? Do we burn with envy and anger because we are not able to obtain the gratification, the contentment and the happiness we seek? Do we get frustrated because we cannot obtain even the good things that we so desire?

That is what was happening to me at one time in my life. I was trying to make myself happy. I saw all those good things that I knew I needed, and I was trying to make them happen by my own efforts. No one has any idea how many years I frustrated myself unbearably trying to make my ministry come to pass. It was certainly God's will for me. He had called me to it and had anointed me for it. Yet it was not happening, no matter how much I tried.

It is interesting that God will call a person to do something, and then not allow him to do it for a while. And he will never be able to do it, until he stops trying to do it on his own and starts allowing the Lord to bring it to pass in His own way and in His own time. God's ways are perfect! If you are frustrated about timing, learn to pray with the psalmist, **My times are in Your hands...**(Ps. 31:15).

I know about these things, because they were exactly what happened to me. I was frustrated and envious and angry and unable to obtain the gratification, contentment and happiness I sought — until the Lord showed me the last sentence in verse 2 of James 4: **...You do not have, because you do not ask.**

When I really saw and understood this sentence for the first time, it jarred my entire theology. It was an important part of the revelation of grace that the Lord gave me that eventually changed my whole life and ministry.

The Lord convicted me of various things in my life. Some of them you may relate to in your own Christian walk. Let me give you an example.

One day I woke up with a throbbing headache. I thought maybe I was catching a cold. I walked around with that miserable headache almost all day, telling everybody I met about how terrible I felt — until finally the Lord spoke to me and said, "Did it ever occur to you to ask Me to heal you?" I believed in Jesus as my healer, but I spent the day complaining and never once asked.

That happens so often in our lives. We go around complaining about our problems and spending half our time trying to figure out what we can do to solve them. We do everything under the sun except the one thing we are told to do in the Word of God: ask, that we may receive that our joy may be full. (John 16:24 KJV.)

Why are we like that? Because the flesh, our carnal human nature, wants to do things itself. That is the nature of the flesh. It wants to conquer. It wants to overcome its own problems in its own way. Why? So it can get the glory. The flesh wants to do it itself, because it wants the credit.

That is one reason we are not more successful than we are in our walk of faith: because we are trying to obtain by our efforts what God wants to give us by His grace. But in order for Him to give us what we need, we must be humble enough to quit trying and start trusting. We must be willing to stop doing and start asking.

Receive, Not Get

[Or] you do ask [God for them] and yet fail to receive, because you ask with wrong purpose and evil,

**selfish motives. Your intention is [when you get what
you desire] to spend it in sensual pleasures.**

James 4:3

In this study I hope to eradicate the word *get* from our
vocabulary and replace it with the word *receive.* These are
two different things.

James tells us that rather than setting out to acquire the
things we need or desire, we are to ask for them. But then
he goes on to say that often the reason we do not receive
what we ask for is because we ask with the wrong motive or
intention.

Sometimes the thing we are asking God for is not wrong
in itself, but He cannot grant our request yet because He
still has some work to do in us to prepare us for it.

For example, it was right for me to seek the Lord about
the ministry to which He had called me. It was the Lord's
will that it succeed. However, even though He had called
me, the first several years of my ministry were difficult ones
because my motives were wrong. Instead of simply
submitting myself to the Lord in humble service to Him, I
was trying to be important. I was insecure and wanted a
high position in the Kingdom of God for wrong reasons.
Until I learned to allow Him to do His own work in me, He
could not work through me. My motives had to be purified,
and that type of change does not take place overnight.

For years I was frustrated because I prayed and fasted
and sought the Lord, and yet nothing happened — at least
very little that I could see. I did not appreciate the value of
the inner work that must be done to prepare us for visible
blessings. I wanted to move in the full flow of God's Spirit,
but there was just a little trickle of the Spirit in my life and
ministry. I could not understand what was wrong.

It even got to the point that I wanted to tell the Lord to
just leave me alone so I could forget about the ministry and

go do something else. I was ready to give up the whole thing.

That happens to many of us. God comes along and starts a work in us and through us. He gets us somewhere out in the middle of what He is doing, and then it seems that He just will not go ahead and finish it. That is where the frustration begins, because we try so hard to move things along, and it is like attempting to move a mountain out of the way with sheer physical force. It just won't work! God, of course, always finishes what He starts, but the waiting helps us get truly rooted and grounded in Him.

Many times this kind of thing happens because our motives are wrong. Sometimes even our motives for seeing our loved ones saved can be selfish. We want them saved not because we love them and want to see them blessed, but because we want our lives to be made easier or better. We want them saved not for their own sake, but so we won't have to put up with their sinful attitudes and behavior.

That is part of what James is talking about when he says that we ask for the wrong purpose or with the wrong intention. Often God knows that our motives and intentions are wrong, even if we don't realize it or won't admit it. It is hard to face the truth about ourselves. But we have to do that if we want to be able to receive all that God desires to give us.

Over the years I have learned one important truth: *God knows me much better than I know myself.* I have come to see that if I ask the Lord for something, and He does not give it to me right away, it is simply because I am not yet ready to receive it.

The Lord once told me, "Joyce, any time you ask Me for something good and you don't get it, it's not because I'm trying to hold out on you or keep you from receiving it.

Either it's because I have something better in mind and you just don't know enough to ask Me for it, so I have to make you wait until you catch up with My plan, or it's because you are out of My timing."

Often it is not a matter of being out of God's will, it is a matter of being out of God's timing. We have not because we ask not. But we also have not because we ask with the wrong motives and intentions, or because we are not yet ready to receive what God wants to give us.

I have learned that when I ask the Lord for something I must make my request and then leave it alone. If it is His will that I receive what I have asked for, He will provide it — in His own way, and in His own time. Waiting does not have to be frustrating if we learn more about God's grace.

Like Unfaithful Wives

You [are like] unfaithful wives [having illicit love affairs with the world] and breaking your marriage vow to God! Do you not know that being the world's friend is being God's enemy? So whoever chooses to be a friend of the world takes his stand as an enemy of God.

James 4:4

What does James mean when he says that we are "like unfaithful wives?" I believe the Lord has given me a good example from my own personal experience.

In my kitchen there are some windows above the sink that are hard for me to reach. Now, when I go to open or close those windows I can jump up on the counter and make a big ordeal out of it. Or I can save myself the struggle and strain by simply calling my husband, Dave, and asking him to come open or close them for me. Dave is much taller than I am, so with his long arms it is no problem for him to do what would be a real frustrating challenge for me.

That is the way we are with the Lord. We struggle and strain, wearing ourselves out trying to do something that the Lord could do for us with no effort at all — if we would just ask Him.

But do you know what would insult my husband even more than refusing to let him help me? Running to the next-door neighbor and asking him to come over and open or close my windows for me. That is the kind of thing James is referring to here in this verse when he talks about our being "like unfaithful wives" who turn to other men for help rather than calling upon our own husband, a symbol of the Lord.

I was frustrated in my life and ministry until I learned to quit either trying to do everything on my own or running to others with my problems rather than running to God.

Grace Defined

Or do you suppose that the Scripture is speaking to no purpose that says, The Spirit Whom He has caused to dwell in us yearns over us and He yearns for the Spirit [to be welcome] with a jealous love?

But He gives us more and more grace (power of the Holy Spirit, to meet this evil tendency and all others fully). That is why He says, God sets Himself against the proud and haughty, but gives grace [continually] to the lowly (those who are humble enough to receive it).

James 4:5,6

As I was reading this passage some years ago searching for the answer to why I was so frustrated and so powerless to overcome my sins and failures, my eyes began to open when I came to verse 6 which says that God gives us "more and more grace." Then *The Amplified Bible* version tells us what grace is.

Before the Lord opened my eyes to this revelation, the only definition I had ever heard of the word *grace* was "undeserved favor." That is good, but there is so much more to grace than that. *The Amplified Bible* says that grace is the power of the Holy Spirit to meet the evil tendency within each of us.

What evil tendency is James referring to here? The evil tendency to be like an unfaithful wife, the evil tendency to have illicit love affairs with the world, the evil tendency to turn away from God and look to ourselves or to others rather than simply asking Him to meet our needs. That is a tendency of the flesh, and it is not the way God wants us to react.

The answer I was seeking is found in verse 6, which tells us that in the midst of all our problems and frustrations God gives us more and more grace, more and more power of the Holy Spirit to meet this evil tendency and all others fully. That is why God sets Himself against the proud and the haughty who think they can handle things on their own without Him, but gives grace continually to the lowly, to those who are humble enough to receive His grace by simply asking for it.

God wants to help us meet every evil tendency within us. He wants to give us His grace. He wants to give us the power to overcome our wrong motives and intentions, if we will be humble enough to ask for it and receive it rather than trying to handle everything ourselves by our own power and in our own way.

Saved by Grace, Living by Works

For it is by free grace (God's unmerited favor) that you are saved (delivered from judgment and made partakers of Christ's salvation) through [your] faith. And this [salvation] is not of yourselves [of your own doing, it came not through your own striving], but it is the gift of God;

> Not because of works [not the fulfillment of the
> Law's demands], lest any man should boast. [It is not
> the result of what anyone can possibly do, so no one
> can pride himself in it or take glory to himself.]
>
> Ephesians 2:8,9

This passage is obviously referring to salvation. But the
Bible says that the way you and I are saved — by grace
through faith — is the way we must live our daily lives. **For
it is by free grace (God's unmerited favor) that you are
saved (delivered from judgment and made partakers of
Christ's salvation) through [your] faith. And this
[salvation] is not of yourselves [of your own doing, it
came not through your own striving], but it is the gift of
God...**(v. 8). The same principles we apply to receive
salvation we must apply to receive every other blessing that
comes from God.

How were we saved? By grace through faith. One of the
things I want to help you learn in this study is the vital
difference between these two words *by* and *through*. That
difference will help keep in proper perspective the different
roles and functions of grace and faith.

Over the past few years we have heard a great deal
about faith. At the time the Lord was opening my eyes to
the truth that I am sharing with you in these pages, I was
very busy trying to have faith, trying to believe God for a
lot of things. I was trying to believe Him for a breakthrough
in my ministry, for the healing of my back, for more
financial prosperity and for my husband and children to
change to what I thought they should be. I "had my faith
out there" — or so I thought. The only problem was that
what I was exercising could not have been faith because I
had no peace of mind and heart, no rest.

The writer of Hebrews tells us, **For we who have
believed (adhered to and trusted in and relied on God) do
enter that rest...**(Heb. 4:3). According to the Bible, once you

and I have believed God (which is what faith is), then we enter His rest. But I had no rest. The reason why I had no rest is simple. Instead of exercising faith in God, I was actually exercising faith in faith. I was worshipping a thing (faith) rather than worshipping a Person (God).

The reason I had fallen into this trap was because I had my hope fixed in my faith rather than in my Lord. I thought that faith was the price we paid for the blessings of God, or another way to say it is, I thought I could *get* what I wanted and needed with my faith. But that thinking is incorrect. God's blessings cannot be *bought* by faith or by anything else, they must be *received*. Faith is not the price that buys God's blessing, it is the hand that receives His blessing. The price that buys everything God wants to give us was paid for us by Jesus Christ on the cross of Calvary. Our salvation was not purchased by our faith but by the shed blood of the Son of God. We simply received that salvation by the grace of God through our faith — that is, by believing (adhering to, trusting in and relying on) God, Who freely gives us all good things to enjoy. (1 Tim. 6:17 KJV.)

The Bible tells us that it is *by* grace *through* faith that you and I are saved and made partakers of God's blessings. It also tells us that the same way we are saved is the same way we are to live and regulate our daily lives.

It is curious that we come to God through Christ, just as we are, relying on nothing but the blood of Jesus to cleanse us from our sins. We are so grateful to God for saving us and giving us eternal life with Him. Why? Because we know that we do not deserve it. But from that moment on, we want to deserve everything else He gives us. From that time forward, God has got to practically force every single blessing upon us. Why? Because we think we don't deserve it. We didn't read the Bible enough today, we didn't pray enough today, we didn't operate in the fruit of the Spirit enough today, we yelled at one of the kids, we kicked the cat, we weren't very nice when we got caught in that traffic jam. We think of everything we did wrong and figure that it automatically disqualifies us for any of God's blessings.

If God could bless only perfect people, then He could never bless anyone, because we have all sinned and come short of the glory of God. (Rom. 3:23 KJV.) None of us deserves any good thing from the Lord. That fact did not keep us from freely receiving His glorious salvation; why should it keep us from receiving His manifold blessings? The reason is that once we are saved by grace through faith, we immediately make the mistake of turning from living by grace to living by works.

Works Versus Grace

Do you understand now why we get so frustrated? It is because with all our emphasis on faith, we are trying to live by *works* a life that was brought into being and designed by God to be lived by *grace.*

Let me give you a practical tip on how grace can be of benefit to you in your everyday life. When you get into a situation that begins to cause you to become frustrated, just stop and say, "O Lord, give me grace." Then believe that God has heard your prayer and is answering that prayer and working out that situation, even as you go about your daily routine.

You see, faith is the channel through which you and I receive the grace of God to meet our needs. If we try to do things on our own without being open to receive the grace of God, then no matter how much faith we may have we will still not receive what we are asking of God. Because the Bible says that grace is the power of God coming to us through our faith to meet our need.

A long time ago I wrote up this statement and stuck it on my refrigerator:

Works of the Flesh = Frustration.

If you can learn this principle — that every time you become frustrated, it is a sign that you have stopped receiving the grace of God — you will soon overcome your evil tendency to become frustrated.

If you are frustrated, it is because you are trying to make things happen on your own. It is not because you don't have any faith; it is because you have stopped receiving from God His grace. I know, because I was totally frustrated about faith. I was trying to get things and do things by faith, and it was simply not working because I was leaving out grace.

Not long ago I found myself in a situation in which I became very tense and "uptight." That is always a sign that I am in a situation I don't know how to handle. I don't want things to be as they are, but I don't have the power to change them.

The more I tried to figure out what to do to solve my dilemma, the more confused, upset and frustrated I became. Finally, I remembered what I am sharing with you in this book — the grace of God. So I stopped and prayed, "Lord, I must not be receiving Your grace; otherwise I would not be frustrated. Father, give me grace."

I sat there in silence and in just a few moments the Lord gave me an answer to my situation. It was so simple I don't know why I didn't see it to begin with. All I could say was, "Thank You, Lord!"

Do you know why we get so frustrated? It is because we want things to be a certain way, and in this life everything just does not always work out the way we want it to, the way we have planned for it to work. That is why we need to trust in and rely on the grace of God. He knows what we are facing in every situation of life, and He will work out things for the best, if we will trust Him enough to allow Him to do so.

Pride Produces Frustration

Likewise, ye younger, be subject to the elder; yea, all of you gird on the lowly mind to serve one another; because "God resisteth the proud, but giveth grace to the lowly."

1 Peter 5:5 WORRELL

Let's look at this verse in the more detailed version of *The Amplified Bible:*

Likewise, you who are younger and of lesser rank, be subject to the elders (the ministers and spiritual guides of the church) — [giving them due respect and yielding to their counsel]. Clothe (apron) yourselves, all of you, with humility [as the garb of a servant, so that its covering cannot possibly be stripped from you, with freedom from pride and arrogance] toward one another. For God sets Himself against the proud (the insolent, the overbearing, the disdainful, the presumptuous, the boastful) — [and He opposes, frustrates, and defeats them], but gives grace (favor, blessing) to the humble.

In both versions we see that God sets Himself against the proud, but gives grace to the humble.

In my situation, as long as I sat there trying to figure out my problem for myself, I was being proud. It is always pride that is our motivator when we try to handle our own situations rather than humbling ourselves and asking God what we ought to do — and then being obedient enough to do what He says, whether we agree with it or not, whether we like it or not.

It really didn't matter whether I liked the plan that God gave me or not; the point was, it worked. There is quite a difference between trying to use what we think is faith to

31

make our plans work and relying on grace to allow God to work out His plan. It is the difference between pride and humility, between frustration and rest. Remember that true faith brings us into rest, but works of the flesh bring frustration.

For a long time in my life, whenever I got frustrated I would blame my frustration on the devil. I would say, "Satan, I rebuke you in the name of Jesus!" But it wasn't the devil who was frustrating me; it was God!

"Now wait a minute," you may be thinking. "That can't be so; it's not scriptural."

Oh, but it is. Right here in *The Amplified Bible* version of 1 Peter 5:5 we read that God opposes, *frustrates*, and defeats the proud, the insolent, the overbearing, the disdainful, the presumptuous, the boastful. Who are these people? They are the ones who try to figure out everything for themselves, those who try to do it their way rather than God's way. They are the ones who try to change themselves into what they think they ought to be rather than asking God to bring about within them the changes that He desires to make.

The Bible says that God opposes us when we act in pride. Why? Because He knows that if He allows us to do things our way, we will never learn to lean on Him. When He opposes us, or hinders *our plan* from working, we feel frustrated.

On the other hand, God gives grace (favor, blessing) to the humble, to those who adhere to, trust in and rely on Him and not on their own ability, schemes and devises — or even on their own great wisdom, knowledge and faith.

Therefore Humble Yourselves

Therefore humble yourselves [demote, lower yourselves in your own estimation] under the mighty hand of God, that in due time He may exalt you.
1 Peter 5:6

Do you know what it means to humble yourself under the mighty hand of God that in due time He may exalt you? It means to ask the Lord for what you need and then wait on Him to provide it as He sees fit, knowing that His timing is always perfect. It means to be still and know that He is God, and that He knows what is best for you in every situation of life. It means to stop trying to make things happen yourself and to allow the Lord to show you what you need to do to cooperate with His plan and purpose for you.

Grace and Worry

Casting the whole of your care [all your anxieties, all your worries, all your concerns, once and for all] on Him, for He cares for you affectionately and cares about you watchfully.

1 Peter 5:7

The person who really understands the grace of God will not worry. Do you know why? Because worry is a work of the flesh. It is trying to figure out what to do to save oneself rather than trusting in God for deliverance.

The individual who is living in constant worry is not receiving the fullness of God's grace, because just as perfect love casts out fear (1 John 4:18 KJV), so God's grace expels all traces of anxiety.

Walk in the grace of the Lord and you will not fulfill the works of the flesh.

Grace and Stability

Be well balanced (temperate, sober of mind), be vigilant and cautious at all times; for that enemy of yours, the devil, roams around like a lion roaring [in fierce hunger], seeking someone to seize upon and devour.

Withstand him; be firm in faith [against his onset — rooted, established, strong, immovable, and

determined], knowing that the same (identical) sufferings are appointed to your brotherhood (the whole body of Christians) throughout the world.

1 Peter 5:8,9

Up to this point Peter has been telling us that if we have a problem, we are to get God involved in it. He has been saying that we are to humble ourselves under the mighty hand of God, refusing to worry or to be anxious but instead to wait upon the Lord, allowing Him to work out His perfect solution in His perfect timing.

Now in this passage he gives us a warning. While we are waiting on the Lord, we must remain steadfast against the devil, our enemy who is out to devour us. Peter exhorts us to be firm in faith, rooted, established, strong, immovable and determined as we stand our ground in faith and trust, leaning not on our own strength but on the strength and power of the Lord.

Lean on God

For we have heard of your faith in Christ Jesus [the leaning of your entire human personality on Him in absolute trust and confidence in His power, wisdom, and goodness] and of the love which you [have and show] for all the saints (God's consecrated ones).

Colossians 1:4

According to the Bible, faith is the leaning of the entire human personality on God in absolute trust and confidence in His power, wisdom and goodness.

Do you know what that says to me? It says that faith is my leaning totally on God, taking all the weight off myself and placing everything on Him, trusting in: 1) His power and ability to do *what* needs to be done, 2) His wisdom and knowledge to do it *when* it needs to be done, and 3) His goodness and love to do it the *way* it needs to be done.

34

Do you have faith enough to lean your entire personality on God, trusting everything you are and have totally and completely on Him? Or do you lean on Him but keep your weight under you also so if He should move, you can quickly regain your balance and stand on your own two feet?

One time in a meeting I pretended to pass out, and my husband had to grab me up in his arms and carry me. If he had dropped me, I would have fallen flat on the floor. I did this to show people how real faith operates. It totally leans on God.

That is faith — letting go and letting God.

Grace and Trusting God

For even to this were you called [it is inseparable from your vocation]. For Christ also suffered for you, leaving you [His personal] example, so that you should follow in His footsteps.

He was guilty of no sin, neither was deceit (guile) ever found on His lips.

When He was reviled and insulted, He did not revile or offer insult in return; [when] He was abused and suffered, He made no threats [of vengeance]; but He trusted [*Himself* and *everything*] to Him Who judges fairly.

1 Peter 2:21-23

When a person trusts everything, including his very life, into the hands of the Lord, that is faith.

Jesus acted in faith while He was being reviled and insulted, even though He was not delivered right away. Earlier He had suffered agony in the Garden of Gethsemane when His disciples let Him down; He couldn't even find anyone to watch and pray with Him for one hour. The Bible says that He prayed so intently that **...His sweat became like great clots of blood dropping down upon the ground**

35

(Luke 22:44). Later, after His trial, He suffered on the way to Calvary. After being ridiculed and beaten and spat upon, He was forced to carry His cross to Golgotha where He was to die in agony. Yet through it all Jesus trusted in God, although there was no deliverance for Him yet. That would come later, after His death and burial.

An Attitude of Faith and Trust

For You will not abandon my soul, leaving it helpless in Hades (the state of departed spirits), nor let Your Holy One know decay or see destruction [of the body after death].

Acts 2:27

This verse is a prophetic utterance that came forth from King David, but it refers to the Messiah. This was the attitude of Jesus, the attitude of faith and trust in His Father that carried Him through the hard times He had to face.

Did you know that it is our faith and trust in the Lord that carries us through the hard times, as we wait patiently for the grace of God to work out our deliverance? Although faith is important, it is not the actual power that delivers; it sustains us until God's power — in the form of grace — arrives on the scene to set us free.

When we say that we are believing God for something to happen, we also need to be praying to the Lord, saying, "Father, I need Your grace. I need Your power to come and deliver me." Remember, our victories come "by grace, through faith."

Often we are told that we must keep our faith on the line, that we must keep believing that what we need we are going to get by faith. But if we are not careful we can get our eyes fastened on the blessing rather than on the Lord. There is a fine line here. We must be very careful that we seek the

Lord's face and not His hand. He wants us to seek Him, and not just what He can do for us.

The same is true in regard to faith and grace. We can focus so much on believing that we begin to worship — adhere to, trust in and rely on — our faith rather than the Lord, the One on Whom our faith is based. Instead of keeping our eyes on the things we are seeking, we need to keep them on God. We need to look beyond our faith to God's grace and say, "Father, I need You to come through my faith by Your grace to bring me what I need."

Often we get so wrapped up in saying "I'm believing God, I'm believing God, I'm believing God" that we become legalistic and do what Paul warned us against — we frustrate the grace of God: **[Therefore, I do not treat God's gracious gift as something of minor importance and defeat its very purpose]; I do not set aside and invalidate and frustrate and nullify the grace (unmerited favor) of God...(Gal. 2:21).** If we place too much emphasis on *our* faith — on *our* belief and *our* faithfulness — then we frustrate God's grace which is based not on *our* works but upon *His* unmerited favor toward us.

We must learn to lean totally upon the Lord, freely acknowledging that it is not by faith but by grace that we receive any of the good things that He wants us to have. We must remember that the most important thing in receiving God's blessings is not *our* great faith but *His* great faithfulness.

God's Faithfulness

You have made known to me the ways of life; You will enrapture me [diffusing my soul with joy] with and in Your presence.

Brethren, it is permitted me to tell you confidently and with freedom concerning the patriarch David that he both died and was buried, and his tomb is with us to this day.

Being however a prophet, and knowing that God had sealed to him with an oath that He would set one of his descendants on his throne,

He, foreseeing this, spoke [by foreknowledge] of the resurrection of the Christ (the Messiah) that He was not deserted [in death] and left in Hades (the state of departed spirits), nor did His body know decay or see destruction.

This Jesus God raised up, and of that all we [His disciples] are witnesses.

Being therefore lifted high by and to the right hand of God, and having received from the Father the promised [blessing which is the] Holy Spirit, He has made this outpouring which you yourselves both see and hear.

Acts 2:28-33

Here we see how Peter told the crowd assembled in Jerusalem on the Day of Pentecost that what they were witnessing that day was the direct result of God's faithfulness to keep His Word to raise up Jesus from the dead and to pour out His Spirit upon all mankind.

Jesus exercised faith and trust in His Father to do what He had promised He would do. And He was not disappointed. His Spirit was not deserted in Hades nor was His body left to rot in the tomb. Instead, He was lifted up and made to sit at the right hand of God in the heavens from which He poured forth the promised Holy Spirit.

Like Peter, it is permitted to me to tell you confidently and with freedom that if you are leaning on God, you will not be deserted in your problem or left to rot in your dilemma. Do you remember the Scripture that says that if the same power that raised Christ from the dead dwells in us, it will quicken our mortal bodies? (Rom. 8:11 KJV.) It is not your faith alone that will deliver you; it is the grace of God that will come into your situation, lift you up and seat you in heavenly places, just as it did for Jesus.

How can I be so sure? Because I know God, because I know that **...He Who promised is reliable (sure) and faithful to His word** (Heb. 10:23).

Faith and Grace Work Together

Let me give you an illustration of the way that faith and grace work together to bring us the blessings of God.

In my meetings I often take along a large electric fan which I set up on the speaker's platform. I call up a member of the audience and have her stand in front of the fan, telling her that I am going to cool her off. When the fan doesn't run even though I turn it on, I ask the audience, "What's wrong? Why is this fan not helping this woman?"

Of course, the audience sees right away what's wrong: "It's not plugged in!" they yell.

"That's right," I say, "and that's exactly what's wrong many times when our prayers are not answered."

I go on to explain that we get our eyes on faith (the fan), expecting it to do the work, but we fail to look beyond the fan to the source of power that causes it to work, which is the Lord.

Jesus had faith all the time He was suffering. He had faith while in the Garden of Gethsemane. He had faith before the high priest and Pilate. He had faith when He was being ridiculed, abused and mistreated. He had faith on the way to Golgotha. He had faith while hanging on the cross. He even had faith while His body lay in the tomb; He had absolute faith that God would not leave Him there but would raise Him up, as He had promised. But do you realize that for all His faith, nothing happened until the power of God came forth to bring about the resurrection? His faith kept Him stable until the Father's appointed time for His deliverance.

In my illustration with the fan, I tell the audience, "I can have absolute faith in this fan, but it will not make this woman one bit cooler until it is connected to the source of power. The same is true of faith. We can have all the faith in the world, but it will avail us nothing until it is 'plugged into' the source of power, which is the grace of God. Keep your eyes on God to deliver you — not your faith."

In order to get our needs met, in order to receive anything from the Lord, we must have both faith and grace. It is *by* grace *through* faith that we are saved. And it is *by* grace *through* faith that all of our prayers are answered and all of our needs are met.

Like you, over the past ten years I have heard a great deal about faith. I heard so much, in fact, that I was about to kill myself trying to believe God for stuff without knowing anything about the grace of God. I didn't know how to lean on God, how to rely on the Lord, how to totally trust my heavenly Father in every situation of life. The problem was that I was trusting my faith rather than trusting my God.

If we trust in our faith rather than trusting in God, we will end up frustrated, trying to make things happen that we have no power to make happen. I was trying to believe God for healing and prosperity and a happy family life — and it just wasn't working. And I didn't understand why not. So I tried to believe God more, which only led to more fatigue, frustration, misunderstanding and unhappiness, discouragement and disappointment.

You see, the mistake I was making was trying to make things happen by faith, by believing God. Instead I had to learn to get beyond that to relying on the grace of God. When I did that, when I gave up all my works, then my frustration ceased. I realized that no matter how much faith I had, if God did not come through my faith by His grace to bring me the answers I needed, I was never going to receive anything.

I finally realized that I was frustrated for one simple reason — because I was frustrating the grace of God, which is the power of God. If we frustrate the grace of God, we are going to feel frustrated.

I pray that you are understanding the point I am making. As I said earlier, there is a very fine line here that we often miss, and if we do miss it, our lives become confused when they should be peaceful. I believe I can summarize my years of frustration as a Christian in this statement:

I was trusting *my* faith to meet my needs. When my needs were not met, then I tried to have more faith because I was not seeing beyond *my* faith. Everything seemed to be based on *my* faith when, in reality, every victory is based on God's faithfulness.

I remember one time when I was agonizing over my lack of faith in an area that I needed God's help in. I was busy condemning myself and feeling guilty when the Holy Spirit led me to 2 Timothy 2:13 (KJV), **If we believe not, yet he abideth faithful: he cannot deny himself.**

The Holy Spirit was trying to teach me to get my eyes off my ability to believe and onto God's willingness to meet my need even though I did not have perfect faith.

Remember the man who came to Jesus asking for healing of his son? Jesus told him that all things are possible to those who believe. The man replied, "Lord, I believe! Help my weakness of faith!" or, "help my unbelief," as the *King James Version* says. The man knew his faith was lacking, but he was honest about it, and Jesus healed his son. (See Mark 9:17-24.)

God's grace (power) came on the scene and gave the man what he did not deserve.

2
The Power of Grace

2

The Power of Grace

Now when [the Samaritans] the adversaries of Judah and Benjamin heard that the exiles from the captivity were building a temple to the Lord, the God of Israel,

They came to Zerubbabel [now governor] and to the heads of the fathers' houses and said, Let us build with you, for we seek and worship your God as you do, and we have sacrificed to Him since the days of Esarhaddon king of Assyria, who brought us here.

But Zerubbabel and Jeshua and the rest of the heads of fathers' houses of Israel said to them, You have nothing to do with us in building a house to our God; but we ourselves will together build to the Lord, the God of Israel, as King Cyrus, the king of Persia, has commanded us.

Then [the Samaritans] the people of the land [continually] weakened the hands of the people of Judah and troubled and terrified them in building,

And hired counselors against them to frustrate their purpose and plans all the days of Cyrus king of Persia, even until the reign of Darius [II] king of Persia.

Ezra 4:1-5

In this chapter I would like to share a message with you about mountain-moving grace.

Let's begin our study of the power of grace by examining this scene from the Old Testament book of Ezra. Here we see the two tribes of Judah and Benjamin who have received permission from Cyrus, the king of Persia, to build a temple to the Lord. When the Samaritans hear what is going on, they come to Zerubbabel, the governor, and the other leaders of the people and ask to join them in erecting the temple, because, they claim, they worship the same God.

If you will check, you will discover that although it is true that these Samaritans were worshipping the God of Israel, it was for the wrong reason. They were doing it because, basically, they had been taught to do so to keep evil out of their camp. These people were not Israelites, they were Assyrians who had simply added the Lord God of Israel to the list of other gods they worshipped. While they did worship the One True God, Jehovah, they also kept their false gods and idols.

Since the Israelites were well aware of this fact, they told the Samaritans, their long-time enemies, that they had no part in building a temple to the Lord. When the Samaritans heard this, it made them so angry that they began to do everything in their power to harass and cause trouble for the Israelites, to frustrate their purpose and plans.

Now what should be the reaction of the godly to that kind of opposition and persecution? I believe the answer to that question is a key to enjoying the life of grace that God wills for His people.

If you and I think that we can do anything for God without stirring up trouble for ourselves, we are wrong. Jesus warned us that in this life we will have tribulation. (John 16:33 KJV.) He said that if people hated and persecuted Him, they will also hate and persecute us, because we belong to Him. (John 15:18,20.) We know that we cannot go through life on this earth without encountering some kind of trouble. Yet so often it is trouble that frustrates us and makes us miserable and unhappy.

Often, when people first come to the Lord, they suddenly begin to be attacked in ways that are totally different from anything they have experienced before. Many times they don't understand what is happening to them or why. If they don't have proper instruction in this area, their misunderstanding and frustration can cause them to give up and fall away.

We must remember that the devil is not going to just sit back and allow us to take new ground without putting up a fight. Any time we begin to make progress in building the Kingdom of God, our enemy is going to come against us. Many times the mistake we make is the one I made in my early Christian life — trying to use faith to get to the place where there is total freedom from trouble. I am sure you know by now that it just doesn't work that way.

The purpose of faith is not always to keep us from having trouble; it is often to carry us through trouble. If we never had any trouble, we wouldn't need any faith. Now by saying that, I don't mean that we should expect to have nothing but trouble or that we should accept trouble as our way of life.

In our own experience, my husband Dave and I live in a tremendous amount of victory. But it is because we have learned to stand our ground and back the devil off our property, to drive him out of different areas in our lives. Learning to be stable in hard times is one of the best ways to do this.

Once you have gained a victory over the enemy, you can't just settle back and relax, assuming that everything will stay as it is. You have got to be prepared for a counterattack. It is not enough to win a victory, you have to be prepared to keep the victory you have won.

I often tell people in my seminars that being a victorious Christian is a full-time job, one that never ends. It requires us to be constantly on the alert. Like the Israelites in this story, we must be ready to respond to the trouble caused by our enemy.

What should be our response to trouble? How do we overcome the obstacles that our adversary throws up in our path? How do we move the mountains that block our way? By human effort and struggle? By anger and frustration? By faith alone? By a good confession? By hours of prayer and Bible study?

Let's look at a passage from Zechariah to see what the Word of God has to teach us on this subject.

Grace as Power

And the angel who talked with me came again and awakened me, like a man who is awakened out of his sleep.

And said to me, What do you see? I said, I see, and behold, a lampstand all of gold, with its bowl [for oil] on the top of it and its seven lamps on it, and [there are] seven pipes to each of the seven lamps which are upon the top of it.

And there are two olive trees by it, one upon the right side of the bowl and the other upon the left side of it [feeding it continuously with oil].

Zechariah 4:1-3

Zechariah had a vision in which an angel spoke to him. In this vision he saw a lampstand made of gold with seven lamps upon it. There were seven pipes to the lamps on the stand and two olive trees, one on either side, to feed the lamps continuously with oil.

Now if you are a student of the Word of God, you know that oil represents the Holy Spirit, and the Holy Spirit is the power of Almighty God. In Chapter 1 we saw from James 4:6 that the grace of God is the power of the Holy Spirit to meet our evil tendencies. Although it doesn't say it in so many words, that means that grace is the power of God to meet our needs and solve our problems.

For years I did not understand grace, so I was a thoroughly frustrated Christian. As I have said, I was constantly trying to accomplish everything in my life by myself. I was struggling to move mountains out of my way by my own human effort.

If I had been in the place of Zerubbabel and the Israelites, I would have worn myself out trying to build a temple for the Lord. I would have known in the depths of my heart that the Lord had told me to erect that building. Since I am such a determined person, I would have worked myself to a frazzle trying to do by my own efforts what the Lord had given me to do.

I would also have been terribly frustrated because I would have allowed my enemy the devil to cause me constant agony. I would have expended all my strength and energy trying to solve a problem that was simply beyond my ability or power to work out on my own. The only thing I would have produced was a person who was totally worn out, confused and miserable.

I needed a vision like the one being given to Zechariah here in this passage in which the limitless power of God's grace is made manifest.

Not by Might, Nor by Power, But by the Spirit

So I asked the angel who talked with me, What are these, my lord?

Then the angel who talked with me answered me, Do you not know what these are? And I said, No, my lord.

Then he said to me, This [addition of the bowl to the candlestick, causing it to yield a ceaseless supply of oil from the olive trees] is the word of the Lord to

Zerubbabel, saying, Not by might, nor by power, but
by My Spirit [of Whom the oil is a symbol], says the
Lord of hosts.

Zechariah 4:4-6

Here the Lord is speaking to the same people who were
trying to build the temple we just read about in the book of
Ezra. He is telling them how they should react to their
frustrating situation. He is saying to them that their response
to trouble should be to depend not upon their own abilities
or efforts, but upon the limitless power of the Holy Spirit to
meet the issues and resolve the crises they face.

The Power of a Proper Relationship With God

For who are you, O great mountain [of human
obstacles]? Before Zerubbabel [who with Joshua had
led the return of the exiles from Babylon and was
undertaking the rebuilding of the temple, before him]
you shall become a plain [a mere molehill]! And he
shall bring forth the finishing gable stone [of the new
temple] with loud shoutings of the people, crying,
Grace, grace to it!

Zechariah 4:7

The Samaritans who came against the Israelites as they
were building the temple of the Lord had become like a
mountain of human obstacles, frustrating them and
preventing them from doing what God had commanded
them to do.

That may be the situation in which you find yourself
right now as you read these words. You may feel that the
Lord has told you to do something, but that the enemy has
thrown up a mountain in your path to frustrate you and
prevent you from carrying out the Lord's will. If so, I know
just how you feel because that is exactly the way I used to
feel.

The problem is one of perspective.

50

Many times we get so caught up in trying to deal with our enemy by our own strength and effort that we lose sight of our relationship with God.

As strange as it may sound, during the first few years of my ministry I believe I spent more time with Satan than I did with God. What I mean is that by constantly thinking about the devil, talking to him, trying to figure out what he was doing and how I could get him off my case, I was focusing my attention much more on the one who was causing me problems than on the One Who had the power to solve all my problems.

As believers, you and I are not to have our eyes focused on the enemy and his works, but on the Lord and His limitless power. It is such a temptation to get caught up in the problem, to get into reasoning and figuring and worrying. When we do that, we magnify the problem over the Problem-Solver.

In this passage the Lord tells Zechariah that the problem facing the Israelites, although it may appear to be a mountain, is actually a molehill. How would you like for all your mountains to become molehills? They can, if you will do what God is saying here and look not at the problems, but at the Lord and His power.

If God has told you to do something, it is certainly His will not only that you begin it, but also that you finish it. But you will never complete your God-given task if you don't understand grace — the power of the Holy Spirit.

Remember, it is not by power or by might, but by the Spirit that we win the victory over our enemy. We overcome *through* faith, *by* grace.

Faith as a Channel, Not a Source

In Ephesians 2:8,9 we saw that we are saved by grace, through faith. Yes, we need faith. But we must understand that faith is not the power that saves us, it is simply the channel through which we receive the grace of God, which is the power of the Holy Spirit.

In this analogy from Zechariah, faith is the lampstand, but grace is the oil. We can have all the lamps in the world, but if there is no oil fueling them, those lamps will not be able to give forth any light or power.

In Chapter 1, I used the example of an electric fan that has the ability to cool off a person, but only if it is plugged into the power source. That illustration applies to our Christian walk. Many times we end up with a lot of principles, methods and formulas, but no real power. The reason is because all those principles, methods and formulas — like faith — are mere channels through which we receive from God. They are all good, and we need to know about them, but alone they cannot solve our problems.

We need to know about faith. Faith is a wonderful thing. The Bible says that without faith it is impossible to please God. (Heb. 11:6 KJV.) The reason it is so important and so vital is because it is the means through which we receive from God all the good things He wants to provide us. That is why the Lord has spent the past several years training His people in faith. He wants them to get their eyes on Him and learn to believe Him so He can do for and through them what He wants done in the earth.

The same is true of prayer, praise, meditation, Bible study, confession, spiritual warfare and all the other precepts we have been hearing about and engaging in. But in all our spiritual activity, we must be careful that we don't start worshipping — adhering to, trusting in and relying on — these things instead of the Lord Himself.

It is possible to worship our prayer time, our Bible study, our confession, our meditation, our praise, our good works. *It is possible to develop faith in our faith rather than faith in our God.* It is almost frightening because there is such a fine line between the two.

But the thing we must remember is that, as good as all these things are, they are only channels to receiving from the Lord. Like the fan in our illustration, they are of no good to us whatsoever unless they are plugged into the divine power source.

Get Plugged In!

My beloved brother or sister, I submit to you that if you are a frustrated, confused Christian, you are not plugged in. If you are plugged in, if you are at peace within, then you know that it is not by your might or power, but by the Spirit of the Lord.

Every time I begin to get frustrated, the Lord speaks to my heart and says, "Joyce, you're doing it again." What am I doing? I am trying to do what only He can do. I am trying to make things happen by my own strength and effort — and becoming frustrated and confused in the process. I am trying to move mountains by my human effort, and I should be saying, "Grace, grace to the mountain."

Frustration is not part of our divine inheritance, and neither is confusion. Like the fan in our illustration, we will never accomplish anything unless we are plugged into the divine power source. How do we stay plugged in? We do that through a personal relationship with God — which requires time.

No matter how many principles and formulas you and I learn, we will never have any real lasting victory in our Christian life without spending time in personal, private fellowship with the Lord. The victory is not in methods; it is in God. If we are to live victoriously, we are going to have to look beyond ways to eliminate our problems and find the Lord in the midst of our problems.

Our heavenly Father knows that none of us can handle the situations we face continually in our daily life without the abiding presence and power of His Holy Spirit.

None of us can do what someone else is doing (just because we would like to), because we are all different. We have different callings, different gifts, different personalities and different lifestyles. Each of us must be with the Lord and allow Him to direct and guide us, telling us what we are to do in each of the situations we encounter as individuals.

God has a personalized plan for each of us, a plan that will lead us to victory. That is why principles, formulas and methods are not the ultimate answer, because they do not allow for the individual differences in people. As good as all these things may be as general guidelines, they are no substitute for personal fellowship with the Living God.

Fellowshipping With God

I know you want peace and victory in your life. How do I know? I know because you are reading this book. That is why I am pointing you toward the Source of all peace and victory — which is not the things of God, but God Himself.

If the devil tries to keep people out of anything, it is fellowship with the Lord. Satan doesn't care how many lamps we have, as long as we don't have any oil to fuel those lamps. He isn't worried about how many fans we have, as long as those fans are never connected to the power source because he knows that once we get to the source of divine power, it is all over for him.

Do you know what happens when you spend time with God? You begin to act like David when he faced the giant

Goliath. You begin to take a stand and demand of the enemy, "Who do you think you are to defy the army of the Living God?" (1 Sam. 17:26.)

As soldiers of the Cross, you and I are not supposed to be afraid of our enemy, the devil. Instead, we are to **...be strong in the Lord, and in the power of his might** (Eph. 6:10 KJV). When a spirit of fear comes along, rather than shaking like a leaf, we are to be as bold as a lion.

The devil comes against those who are doing damage to his kingdom, those who are doing something for God. How do we withstand the devil? By girding on the full armor of God, taking up the shield of faith, by which we can quench all his fiery darts, and by wielding the sword of the Spirit, which is the Word of God. (Eph. 6:13-17 KJV.) But all of that armor and all of those weapons come from spending time in fellowship with the Lord.

Ephesians 6:10 actually begins this discourse on the armor of God, saying, **...be strong in the Lord [be empowered through your union with Him]....** To me, that says, "Be strong through your fellowship with God." Then verse 11 goes on to say, **Put on God's whole armor....** Only after being strengthened in fellowship can we properly wear the armor.

In my own case, I have learned to discipline myself to spend several hours each day in personal fellowship with my heavenly Father. The Lord has told me that there is no way that I can have a successful Christian life and ministry if I am not willing to give a hundred percent of myself to Him.

If I want victory, I have no choice; I have to fellowship with the Lord several hours every day — because of the call that is on my life. The Lord may not require that kind of commitment from you. He may require of you only an hour a day, maybe thirty minutes in the morning and thirty minutes at night. It may be more or it may even be less; the exact amount varies from person to person. But whatever the amount of actual time you are called upon to spend with the Lord daily, I can tell you that if you are not willing to make that sacrifice, you can forget about being victorious and enjoying peace in your Christian life. You will still make it to heaven, of course, because your name is written in the Lamb's Book of Life. Salvation is not based on your fellowship — it is based on the blood of Jesus. But you will struggle the entire time you are here on this earth.

You and I must learn that it is only in the *presence* of the Lord that we receive the *power* of the Lord.

When I first started trying to spend time with God, it was hard for me. I felt silly and self-conscious. I was bored. I would sit and yawn and try not to fall asleep. Like anything worthwhile, sitting quietly in the presence of the Lord takes time to master. You have to keep at it. And it is not something that you can learn from someone else. I don't think it is possible to teach another human being to fellowship with God. Why? Because each person is different and has to learn for himself how to communicate with his Creator.

My fellowship time includes prayer of all kinds (petition, intercession, praise, etc.), reading books that God is using to help me, Bible study, waiting on God, repentance, crying, laughing, receiving revelation. My time with Him is different almost every day.

God has an individual plan for each person. If you will go to Him and submit to Him, He will come into your heart and commune with you. He will teach and guide you in the way you should go. Don't try to do what someone else does or to be what someone else is. Just allow the Lord to show you how you are to fellowship with Him. Then follow as He directs your life, step by step.

Sometimes you may have to store up oil for the future. That is, not only must you spend time in fellowship with the Lord day by day, but there will be occasions when you will have to spend more time than usual because the Lord knows that you are facing a situation that is going to put a drain on your physical and spiritual resources.

Do you remember the parable Jesus told about the ten virgins who brought their lamps and came to wait for the bridegroom to arrive? Five of them were foolish and brought only enough oil for the moment, while the other five were wise enough to bring extra oil in case the bridegroom was delayed. When the bridegroom arrived late, those who had run out of oil begged the others to lend them some of theirs, but they refused. Because the foolish virgins had to hurry out to buy some more oil, they missed the wedding feast. (Matt. 25:1-12.)

Isn't that the way some of us are? We won't take the time and trouble to prepare for what is to come. We run out of oil and try to borrow from those who have extra. The Lord may allow that for a while, but sooner or later each of us must learn to store up for ourselves reserves of oil for future occasions.

If you will give up fifteen or twenty minutes of sleep in the morning in order to get up early and seek His face, God will honor that sacrifice. If you are willing to turn off the television for thirty minutes in the evening and spend some time in fellowship with the Lord, you will be richly rewarded.

There are times when hard work or a trying situation has drained all your reserves and you need "extra time" to replenish what you have used up.

That doesn't mean that you are never going to be able to have any fun or that you will be sitting in a room with God all the time. He is a loving Father. He wants His children to have an abundant and enjoyable life. He is not going to require more of you than what you are able to give Him. He is not an ogre Who is out to make you miserable. He just knows what you need in order to have that abundant, enjoyable, victorious life. He also knows that it doesn't come from methods, but from Him.

Learn to quickly follow the promptings of the Holy Spirit. *Come apart with Him privately before you come apart publicly.* Spend time with God so you can remain stable as you deal with the daily affairs of life.

Not by Effort, But by Spirit

The devil wants you and me to think that we can buy the grace of God. God's grace is not for sale, because by its very definition — *unmerited* favor — it is a gift.

Grace cannot be bought by prayer, good works, Bible reading or offerings. It cannot be bought by reading, memorizing or confessing Scriptures. It cannot even be bought by faith. The grace of God is receivable, but it is not "buyable."

Before the Lord got hold of me and began to change me from the inside out, I was terrible. I did not have the fruit of the Spirit in me. Instead I manifested the fruit of the flesh: I was impatient, sharp, rude, unmannerly, selfish, self-centered, greedy, hard to get along with — and on and on. Even though I am now saved and baptized in the Holy Ghost, even though I love God and long to serve Him with my whole heart, if I did not spend time with Him every day as I do, I would still act the way I used to act.

We Christians must learn the sad fact that our salvation experience does not make us act any better than we ever did. We must renew our minds with God's Word and spend time with the Holy Spirit. If we want to act better, we have got to be plugged into the Spirit of the Living God. This is the lesson that the Lord taught me in my own life and ministry. If I want to shine, I must stay plugged in.

After struggling for years as a Christian and a preacher, I finally got it through my head that it is not by my might or power, but it is by the Spirit of the Lord that I am to live. The success of my life and ministry does not depend upon my effort, but upon the presence and power of the One Who lives His life in me and through me. (Gal. 2:20 KJV.)

When I stand in front of people in a meeting, especially one composed of Christians from all different churches and denominations, I know that no matter how much I may study and prepare, I don't have the power to preach the Word of the Lord to them on my own. I have to rely totally on the grace of the Lord, leaving everything to Him, allowing Him to do in and through me what I cannot do in and of myself. Of course I study and prepare, but even that can fail me, if He doesn't show up.

Sometimes in our zeal to serve the Lord, we do too much. I know there have been times when I was actually overprepared. I studied and prayed for so many hours that I got all caught up in me. Often that is why, despite all our activity, nothing happens. Even when God does show up and work in and through us, sometimes we are not thankful and grateful because we think we earned the results by our own effort.

A Laborer Or a Believer?

Now to a laborer, his wages are not counted as a favor or a gift, but as an obligation (something owed to him).

But to one who, not working [by the Law], trusts (believes fully) in Him Who justifies the ungodly, his faith is credited to him as righteousness (the standing acceptable to God).

Romans 4:4,5

If you and I spend time reading the Bible, praying, meditating, making a positive confession or even being with the Lord, in an effort to get something from Him, then our fellowshipping with Him becomes work rather than grace.

We must be very careful that even when we operate by all the right methods our motives are pure. Let us not fall into the trap of thinking that we *deserve* anything good from the Lord.

According to the Bible, you and I don't deserve anything except to die and spend eternity in everlasting punishment. Why? Because in the Lord's eyes, all of our righteousness, every good thing that we could ever do, is like filthy rags. (Is. 64:6 KJV.)

We need to look upon our righteousness as compared with the righteousness of Almighty God. If we will do that, instead of comparing our righteousness with the unrighteousness of others, then we will see ourselves as we really are. Now I am not talking about feeling bad about ourselves. I am talking about knowing who we are in Christ Jesus, not in our own works or efforts.

As a minister, I don't deserve to enjoy the anointing of the Lord upon my life and work just because I spend time with Him on a daily basis. In addition to spending time with God, I know that I have to have right motives. Along with communing with the Holy Spirit, I have to be in the right spirit myself. Let me illustrate.

There was a time when I was trying to read the entire Bible through in a year. That might sound impressive, but it wasn't, because my motive was all wrong. I wasn't doing it because God was leading me to do so. I was doing it to try to keep up with everyone else in the church.

There was a time when I was trying to pray four hours a day. Do you think the Lord would let me do that? No way!

Every time I would begin to pray, I would fall sound asleep or run out of things to pray about. Do you know why the Lord wouldn't let me pray four hours a day? Because my motive was not right, because I was doing it for the wrong reason. I wasn't doing it because the Lord had led me to do so, but because someone had come to our church and testified about how she prayed four hours a day. So I thought, "Bless God, I'm going to do that too."

I want you to know that determination and will-power can only take you so far. When the flesh fizzles out — and it will — the whole thing will collapse, and so will you.

If we are to serve the Lord, our motives must be right. We are to seek the Lord and to fellowship with Him for no other reason than the fact that we love Him and want to be in His presence. Any time we get to thinking that we deserve something because we are doing something for God — whatever it may be, even spending time with Him — we are following a method rather than the Spirit.

I have learned not to overprepare for meetings. I study and pray as long as God's anointing is on me to do so. When it lifts, I have learned to quit. It took a while (years, in fact) for me to learn that I could not deserve or buy a good meeting with long hours of preparation. Sometimes I study longer than at other times, but at all times I follow Him — not me.

One time when I was preaching this message in a series of meetings, my husband Dave said something very important. He said, "Farmers have formulas for planting, but not for reaping." What he meant was that while people can sow seeds, they can't make them grow and produce a harvest.

When a farmer goes out to sow a crop, he first has to prepare his fields. He has to break up the ground, pull up the grass and weeds, plow the soil up into rows, plant the seeds and then add water and fertilizer. But according to the Bible, no farmer ever makes the seeds germinate and grow.

In the parable of the sower in Mark's Gospel, Jesus likens the Kingdom of God to a farmer who sows his seed in his field and then goes to sleep, and rises night and day, and the seed springs forth and grows up, **...he knoweth not how** (Mark 4:27 KJV).

You see, we don't understand what happens once the seed is placed in the ground. Yes, we are to plant our seed. Prayer is a seed. Bible study is a seed. Preparation is a seed. Meditation is a seed. A good confession is a seed. An offering is a seed. Church attendance is a seed. Good works is a seed. Time spent with God is a seed. But none of these things is a way of purchasing God's grace, because His grace is a gift.

We do not earn God's favor by our labor; we receive it as a gift. God's blessings come upon us not by works but by grace, through faith.

Any time we get wrapped up in self and ego we are on dangerous ground. We must get beyond ourselves and our works and efforts and keep our eyes focused on God and His grace toward us.

Faith in God

And Jesus, replying, said to them, Have faith in God [constantly].

Truly I tell you, whoever says to this mountain, Be lifted up and thrown into the sea! and does not doubt at all in his heart but believes that what he says will take place, it will be done for him.

Mark 11:22,23

Notice that in this passage the first thing Jesus tells us to do is to have faith (constantly) in God — not in our faith or confession.

There was a time in my life when I was so wrapped up in faith and confession that I was convinced that if I said something, it had to happen because I said it. The mistake I made was thinking that it was my faith and my confession that made what I said come to pass. I forgot that in order to receive anything from God I had to put my trust in Him and not in my words or actions. The Lord had to teach me to keep my eyes on Him and not on a method or formula. I believe in confessing the Word. I teach it and do it daily. God works through it, and my faith remains in Him, not my confession.

God Is Able

Now unto him that is able to do exceeding abundantly above all that we ask or think, according to the power that worketh in us.

Ephesians 3:20 KJV

This is such a powerful Scripture. If you will meditate upon it, I think you will see that it is what I call "shouting ground."

What it tells us is that our God is able — able to do far above and beyond anything that you and I can ever dare to hope, ask or even think.

We need to pray, to do the asking. Remember what I said in the early part of the book: "We have not because we ask not." Our job is to do the asking, in faith, in trust. That opens the channel. But it is God Who does the work, not us. How does He do it? **According to** [or by] **the power** [or grace of God] **that worketh in us.**

I sincerely believe that whatever you and I receive from the Lord is directly related to the amount of grace we learn to receive.

We have seen that grace is power. Now I would like to examine how the grace or power of God can be applied to meet specific situations in life. The first thing I would like to discuss is how to receive the grace of God to change ourselves.

Are you struggling with changes that need to be made in your own personality? Do you ever get frustrated and confused, trying to believe and have faith and confess and do all the right things to bring about change in yourself and your life, yet it never seems to happen? Do you end up more frustrated and confused than you were before you started?

As I have told you, that was what was happening to me. I was putting unbelievable stress on myself trying to change. I was under tremendous condemnation because every message I heard seemed to be telling me to change, yet I couldn't change no matter how hard I tried, believed or confessed. I was in a terrible mess because I saw all the things about me that needed to be changed, but I was powerless to bring about those changes.

I don't know about you, but I am a Mrs. Fix-It. Whenever anything is wrong, the first thing I want to do is jump up and set it straight. I wanted to change everything I saw wrong about myself and my life, but for some reason I just couldn't do it. I thought it was the devil who was preventing me. But I learned that it was the Lord Himself Who would not let me change. Why? Because I was trying to do it apart from Him so I could take the credit and the glory that rightfully belonged to Him.

By the time you have finished reading this book, you will have learned at least one thing. You will understand fully why people don't have a thankful, grateful heart. You will see clearly that we humans do not deserve the least of God's blessings. Once you fully understand that truth, then every time something good comes into your life, instead of boasting and taking credit for it because of your great faith or confession or other works, you will automatically respond, "O God, thank You!"

I used to go around asking the Lord, "Father, I did everything right; why didn't it work?" The answer was because I was wrapped up in myself and in what I was doing instead of keeping my attention focused on the Lord and what He was doing for me because of His great mercy, love and grace.

Asking God Versus Doing It Yourself

Let me ask you this one question: Did you receive the [Holy] Spirit as the result of obeying the Law and doing its works, or was it by hearing [the message of the Gospel] and believing [it]? [Was it from observing a law of rituals or from a message of faith?]

Are you so foolish and so senseless and so silly? Having begun [your new life spiritually] with the [Holy] Spirit, are you now reaching perfection [by dependence] on the flesh?

Have you suffered so many things and experienced so much all for nothing (to no purpose) — if it really is to no purpose and in vain?

Then does He Who supplies you with His marvelous [Holy] Spirit and works powerfully and miraculously among you do so on [the grounds of your doing] what the Law demands, or because of your believing in and adhering to and trusting in and relying on the message that you heard?

Galatians 3:2-5

In verse 2 Paul is asking the Galatian believers, "Did you receive the Lord through your own works and efforts or by hearing the Gospel message and saying, 'I believe that?'"

Then in verse 3 he asks them, "Are you really so foolish and senseless and silly as to begin your new life by the Spirit and then try to reach perfection by depending on your own weak human flesh?"

When the Lord was giving me this message, this was one of the Scriptures He revealed to me that had a mighty impact on my life. I saw that I had received the Lord by faith, but I was trying to perfect myself by depending on my own flesh. I was trying to change myself and my life by human effort rather than by trusting totally in Him.

Now, effort has a place in the Christian life. It does have a part to play. But even then, anything done outside the grace of God will have no real lasting effect.

Next Paul asks the Galatians, "Have you suffered all these things for nothing and to no purpose? Do you really want to go back now and start the sanctification process all over again?"

In the early years of my life and ministry, I suffered terribly. Any time we get into works, that is exactly what we will do.

Finally, in verse 5 Paul concludes his argument by asking, "Does God supply your every need and work miracles among you because you keep the Law perfectly or because you put your entire faith and trust in the message you heard?"

It may sound ridiculous, but when I was so frustrated and confused about trying to change myself, it never occurred to me to ask the Lord to change me — and then leave it to Him. I was like someone who talks too much. When the Holy Spirit comes and convicts that person by saying, "You need to learn to be quiet sometimes," what should he do? Instead of arguing or making excuses, he should just say, "You're right, Lord. I do talk too much. You know me, Father. This mouth of mine has been out of control for a long time. I don't think there is any hope of getting it under control without You. Please help me; otherwise, I'm doomed to fail again."

The Lord has to be our Source and our Supply. That is something I had to learn the hard way.

Although I knew that there were many changes that needed to be made in my life, it never occurred to me that God was the only One Who could bring about those changes. I didn't know enough to get on my face before the Lord on a regular basis and say, "Father, I'm out of control. I can't help myself. I am coming to You like a little child. I am totally helpless. I lay this whole situation before You, asking for Your grace. I don't deserve Your help, Father, but You are my only hope. Please do for me what I cannot do for myself."

Many times we will ask for God's help only if we think we have done something to deserve it or earn it. I had to learn to say, "Father, although I am not worthy of Your help, I know that this is not going to work unless You add the power."

If you talk too much, only God can help you. The Bible says in James 3:8 that no man can tame the tongue. Another example would be if you need to lose weight. You can have the right diet, but without the power of God, you will fail time and time again. It may work for everybody else, but not for you. The Lord Himself may even prevent it from working for you — unless you are willing to allow Him to bring about the change and to receive all the credit and the glory.

When are we ever going to learn to ask the Lord instead of trying to do everything for ourselves?

From Glory to Glory

Now the Lord is the Spirit, and where the Spirit of the Lord is, there is liberty (emancipation from bondage, freedom).

And all of us, as with unveiled face, [because we] continue to behold [in the Word of God] as in a mirror the glory of the Lord, are constantly being transfigured into His very own image in ever increasing splendor and from one degree of glory to another; [for this comes] from the Lord [Who is] the Spirit.

2 Corinthians 3:17,18

Notice that our liberty, our emancipation, our freedom from bondage, comes not from ourselves, but from the Spirit of God as we continue to behold the glory of God. As we continue in His Word, *He* changes us. The credit is His, not ours.

The Work Is the Lord's!

And I am convinced and sure of this very thing, that He Who began a good work in you will continue until the day of Jesus Christ [right up to the time of His return], developing [that good work] and perfecting and bringing it to full completion in you.

Philippians 1:6

It is God Who has begun this good work in us. He started it, and He is going to finish it. He is working within us right now, developing, perfecting and bringing to completion the good work which He initiated. Since He is the only One Who can do that, you and I can relax. The pressure is off us, because the work is the Lord's, not ours. I believe this truth will bring us into God's rest. Once we have His rest and peace, we can enter His joy.

Looking to Jesus, Not Ourselves

Looking away [from all that will distract] to Jesus, Who is the Leader and the Source of our faith [giving the first incentive for our belief] and is also its Finisher [bringing it to maturity and perfection]....

Hebrews 12:2

I want to encourage you to keep your eyes off yourself and your troubles and instead to fasten them firmly on

Jesus and His power. He already knows what is wrong with you. He is ready, willing and able to bring about the changes that need to be made in you and your life. He will bring you to maturity and perfection — if you will just ask Him and trust Him to do so.

In my case, I would not go to the Lord with my list of things that were wrong with me. I thought that because of all these terrible things the Lord would (or could) have nothing to do with me until they were all changed.

That is what people do many times. They draw away from God because of their sins and failures and wrongs. When they get into the Word and come under conviction, they actually put distance between themselves and the Lord because they feel so bad about themselves they can't stand to be in His presence. That is a mistake. God's Word convicts us so we will be drawn to Him, not so we will draw away from Him.

I am so grateful and thankful that the Lord didn't push me away because of all my faults. Instead, He drew me to Himself and began to change me into what He wanted me to be. All I had to do was to be willing to be changed, to be sanctified — and to ask and trust Him to do it. Then stay out of "works of the flesh" and wait on Him. We receive the promises through faith and patience. (Heb. 6:12).

To God Be the Glory!

Abstain from evil [shrink from it and keep aloof from it] in whatever form or whatever kind it may be.

And may the God of peace Himself sanctify you through and through [separate you from profane things, make you pure and wholly consecrated to God]; and may your spirit and soul and body be preserved sound and complete [and found] blameless at the coming of our Lord Jesus Christ (the Messiah).

> **Faithful is He Who is calling you [to Himself] and utterly trustworthy, and He will also do it [fulfill His call by hallowing and keeping you].**
> **1 Thessalonians 5:22-24**

Verse 22 is typical of the kind of Scriptures that used to threaten and intimidate me. I would read things like **abstain** (keep away) **from evil** and instantly I had a new job on my hands. I didn't know that the Lord was my Keeper and my Sanctifier; I thought it was my job to keep and sanctify myself, to make myself pure and wholly consecrated and blameless.

In verse 23, the word *sanctify* simply means "to make holy."[1] Who does this? The God of peace Himself.

Notice verse 24 that tells us that God Who called us to Himself is faithful and utterly trustworthy. He will do it! He will do what? He will fulfill His call upon our lives by hallowing (sanctifying) us and keeping us.

This may seem to be a contradiction. First Paul says that we are to abstain from evil, and then in the very next verse he turns right around and says that the Lord will do it for us. In that case, what is our part?

Believing!

That's what I mean when I say that faith is the channel through which we receive the blessings of the Lord. And one of those blessings is sanctification, holiness, purity of mind and heart, the hallowing and keeping of our soul.

Since it is the Lord Who works all these things in us and for us, He wants the glory to go to Him and not to a set of principles, methods or formulas.

That is why we sing, "To God be the glory, great things *He* hath done!"

---

[1]*Webster's New World Dictionary*, 3rd college ed., s.v. "sanctify."

Believers Are Achievers

Stop toiling and doing and producing for the food that perishes and decomposes [in the using], but strive and work and produce rather for the [lasting] food which endures [continually] unto life eternal; the Son of Man will give (furnish) you that, for God the Father authorized and certified Him and put His seal of endorsement upon Him.

They then said, What are we to do, that we may [habitually] be working the works of God? [What are we to do to carry out what God requires?]

Jesus replied, This is the work (service) that God asks of you: that you *believe* in the One Whom He has sent [that you cleave to, trust, rely on, and have faith in His Messenger].

John 6:27-29

I cannot tell you how many times I have said to the Lord, "Father, what do You want me to do? If You will just show me what to do, I'll gladly do it."

I was a doer. All anybody had to do was to show me what needed to be done, and I did it — and I did it right. But what frustrated and confused me was when I did something right, and it still didn't work.

"What must we do to work the works of God?" these people wanted to know. Nobody had told them to work the works of God; that was their idea. God is big enough to work His own works.

That is the way we are. We hear about the mighty works of God, and immediately our reaction is, "Lord, just show me what I can do to work those works."

What was Jesus' answer to these people? "This is the work that God requires of you, that you *believe*."

Now when the Lord first revealed this passage to me, I thought He was going to show me what to do to finally be successful in doing His works. And in a sense He did.

He told me, "Believe."

"You mean that's it?" I asked.

"Yes," He answered, "that's it."

You and I think we are supposed to be achievers, and we are. But the way we achieve is to believe. That frees us from worry and reasoning.

3
Freedom From Worry
and Reasoning

3

Freedom From Worry and Reasoning

Peace I leave with you; My [own] peace I now give and bequeath to you. Not as the world gives do I give to you. Do not let your hearts be troubled, neither let them be afraid. [Stop allowing yourselves to be agitated and disturbed; and do not permit yourselves to be fearful and intimidated and cowardly and unsettled.]

John 14:27

It is obvious from such Scriptures as this one that God wants His children to be free of worry and reasoning.

According to the dictionary, *worry* means to torment oneself with disturbing thoughts; to feel uneasy, anxious or troubled; or, to torment with annoyances, cares or anxieties. This is usually what we have in mind when we talk about worry.

However, there is another dictionary definition of this word that is worth pondering. This one does not have to do with a mental or emotional state or condition, but with a physical activity. *Worry* also means to seize by the throat with the teeth and shake or mangle.

We have all seen a dog or cat grab a smaller animal in its mouth and "worry" or choke it into submission. Applied to the spiritual realm, we have also seen how the devil tries to steal the peace that was left to us by Jesus by seizing us by the throat and shaking and mangling us until we submit.

So worry is not just something we do to ourselves, it is also something our enemy does to us — if we allow it to happen.

The other word we are dealing with in this chapter is *reasoning*. I prefer my own definition to those I have found elsewhere. To me, reasoning is the endless revolving of one's mind around and around a situation, searching for knowledge and understanding.

Isn't that a pretty good description of what happens when you and I get some problem on our mind? When something is bothering us, don't we turn it over and over in our thoughts, endlessly looking for some kind of answer or solution to it?

Although worry is almost always totally negative and pointless because it never produces anything good, sometimes reasoning can *seem* to be positive and productive. We may feel that we have figured out our situation. We may then come into some kind of peace because we think we have worked out a way to handle whatever is bothering us. That is usually a false peace that doesn't last, because we are trying to solve a problem by leaning on our own understanding rather than leaning on the Lord.

Lean on the Lord, Not on Self

Lean on, trust in, and be confident in the Lord with all your heart and mind and do not rely on your own insight or understanding.

In all your ways know, recognize, and acknowledge Him, and He will direct and make straight and plain your paths.

Be not wise in your own eyes; reverently fear and worship the Lord and turn [entirely] away from evil.

Proverbs 3:5-7

When the writer of this Proverb tells us in verse 7 not to be wise in our own eyes, he means that we are not to think that we have the capacity to figure out everything that is going on in our life. You and I don't have the capability to come up with all the answers we need to live victoriously in this world.

Now I have to admit that for most of my life I was a "figure-outer." I was always thinking and reasoning. It wasn't enough for me just to know what God was going to do, I also had to know when and how He was going to do it.

If the Lord did something for me I hadn't expected to happen, I wanted to know how He had done it. If someone blessed me anonymously, I would stay awake at night trying to figure out who that person was who had blessed me.

Finally, one day the Lord gave me a little revelation on this subject. He spoke to me and said, "Joyce, you're not half as smart as you think you are. You think you've got a lot of things figured out, but really you've got them in the wrong slot."

I instantly knew what He was talking about. In my office we had little mail slots for each employee. I would often put a memo in somebody's mail slot, expecting that individual to act on it. Later when I discovered that the person hadn't done what I had requested, I would ask, "Didn't you get the message I put in your slot?" Sometimes I discovered that he or she had not received the message, and it was because I had put it in the wrong slot. God was telling me in that revelation that the same thing was happening in other areas of my life.

The Lord used that example from my own experience to show me that I was spending far too much time and energy worrying and reasoning, trying to figure out and control everything that was going on in my life. He showed me that sometimes we think we have everything figured out and we learn six months or a year down the road that things are not the way we thought they were at all.

That is what the writer of the book of Proverbs is telling us here in this passage when he says that we are to lean not on our own understanding but to lean on, trust in and be confident in the Lord. But how can we tell if we are leaning on ourselves rather than on the Lord?

In Proverbs 16:9 we read: **A man's mind plans his way, but the Lord directs his steps and makes them sure**. It is wisdom to plan our work and then work our plan. Yet we are told that it is God and not our planning that brings success. So where is the balance here?

We know that we are never going to get anything done if we don't have some kind of plan. In Ephesians 5:17 the Apostle Paul warns us, **Therefore do not be vague and thoughtless and foolish, but understanding and firmly grasping what the will of the Lord is**.

Without a plan, we would never finish school, find a job, get married, have children, save up money, buy a car, build a house, take a vacation or do any of the things we do in life. Without a plan, we would not study God's Word, pray, go to church, or do anything to grow in our relationship with God. So there is no argument that we need to plan. The problem is not in our planning, but in our worrying and reasoning.

Beware of Excess

I have a saying that I believe is worth remembering: *Excess is the devil's playground!*

Often our problem is not *normal* planning, but *excessive* planning. Anything out of balance becomes a problem. We get so caught up in details that we lose sight of the big picture. We become so involved in managing every tiny aspect of our daily lives that we forget to live and enjoy life.

And that is excess.

I can give you a simple clue to help you decide whether you have gone from normal planning and preparing to worrying and reasoning: if you get frustrated and confused, you have gone too far. When the Lord gave me this outline for my own life, it really helped me.

Remember, every time you feel frustrated and confused, it is a sign you are out of grace and into works. When you have a problem in your life that you do not know how to handle, what you need is not more figuring and reasoning, but more grace. If you can't see a solution to your problem, then you need the Lord to reveal it to you. The more you worry and reason, the more you fret and strain and turn the problem over in your mind, the more unlikely you are to see the solution to it.

You need to hear from the Spirit, and the more you get in the flesh, the less likely you are to recognize God's answer to your problem. The Word of God says to follow peace. (Heb. 12:14 KJV.) Reasoning does not produce peace. It produces confusion.

The Peace of God

And let the peace (soul harmony which comes) from Christ rule (act as umpire continually) in your hearts [deciding and settling with finality all questions that arise in your minds, in that peaceful state] to which as [members of Christ's] one body you were also called [to live]. And be thankful (appreciative), [giving praise to God always].

Colossians 3:15

What peace it was for me to learn that I don't have to figure everything out. I am happy to say that I have been rescued from reasoning. And if I could be rescued from reasoning, then you can be too, because I was the world's champion reasoner. I had to have a reason for everything. I spent my entire life running my mind, trying to figure out what to do.

You must realize that the flesh enjoys this kind of thing. Of course, certain types of personalities —like mine — are more given to reasoning than others are. Thinkers like to sit around and mull over their problems, trying to work out how to handle them. I certainly did. I started out every day by sitting down with a cup of coffee and fellowshipping with my problems.

Are you fellowshipping with your problems, or with the Lord? Are you into works, or grace?

Grace Versus Works

And if by grace, then is it no more of works: otherwise grace is no more grace. But if it be of works, then is it no more grace: otherwise work is no more work.

Romans 11:6 KJV

What the Apostle Paul is telling us in this verse is simply this: grace and works are diametrically opposed to one another. They cannot fellowship or have anything to do with each other.

Stated another way, grace and works are mutually exclusive. Where one exists, the other cannot exist.

If you and I are into works, then we are out of grace. If we are in grace, then we are out of works. Any time we get into works, the grace of God ceases to operate on our behalf. God has no choice but to back off and wait until we have finished trying to handle things ourselves.

As long as we continue to try to figure out our own problems, we will only get more and more frustrated and confused. The reason is because we are trying to operate without the grace of God — and that is never going to be successful.

In my ministry, the prayer request I receive most often is for guidance. Many people just do not seem to know what to do. They are frustrated and confused by the situations they face in their everyday lives. They need help, and they don't know where to look for it. They need answers, and they don't know where to find them.

I will never forget when the Lord first began to deal with me on this subject. At the time I was really praying and asking God for discernment. Now you must understand that discernment does not come out of the head, but out of the heart, out of "the inner man." (Eph. 3:16 KJV.) Discernment is simply God's wisdom for any situation of life. It is a "spiritual knowing" about how to handle things.

If I have a problem, I don't need to try to figure it out, I need discernment. I need to hear from the Lord. I need God's word on my situation. I need for Him to show me what to do.

As I was praying and asking God for discernment, the Lord spoke to me and said, "Joyce, you are never going to have discernment until you give up reasoning."

Now notice that the Lord didn't say "until I deliver you from reasoning," He said "until you give up reasoning."

If you are trying to figure out everything in life, you must realize that it is just a habit, a bad habit, one that you will have to break. Your mind may be like mine was. As soon as any problem or situation arose, I would immediately try to jump in and figure out a solution to it. If so, you have to break your mind of that kind of habitual reaction.

As I have said, if you are frustrated and confused, it is a sure sign that you are in excess, that you are depending on works rather than on grace.

Confusion is not from God. The Bible says that God is not the author of confusion, but of peace. (1 Cor. 14:33 KJV.) As soon as you begin to feel frustrated and confused, as soon as you start to lose your sense of inner peace, you need to say to yourself, "Uh-oh, I've gone too far." You have to realize that you are out of grace and into works. You must give up your efforts and entrust yourself totally to the Lord, leaving your situation entirely in His hands.

Once you turn from your reasoning to the grace of God, you open a channel of faith through which He can begin to reveal to you what you need to know in order to handle that problem or situation. Enter God's rest, and you will begin to hear His answers.

Remember: worrying and reasoning do nothing but cause more frustration and confusion. You don't need to worry and reason, you need to be quiet and listen. You will never make any real progress in hearing from God until the excessive reasoning is properly dealt with.

What does the Apostle Paul tell us in Romans 11:6? He says that if we are into works, then we are out of the grace of God, because works and grace have nothing to do with each other.

Earlier we studied Zechariah, Chapter 4, in which the Israelites were trying to finish a temple they were building for the Lord. They were asked by the Samaritans to let them join with them in erecting the temple to Jehovah, but their answer was, "No, you have no part with us in this project." That is the attitude you must have toward works: works have no part in grace. You must say, "Works, you have no part in my life. I live by grace."

The Israelites were troubled and frustrated by a mountain of human obstacles. The Lord gave them a word of instruction on how to get that mountain out of their path. He told them, "It is not by might, nor by power, but by My Spirit." (Zech. 4:6.) Later He said, "Say grace, grace to the mountain!" (Zech. 4:7.)

You and I are not to try to wear down the mountain with a hammer, we are to speak to it, crying, "Grace, grace!"

Where works fail, grace always succeeds.

A Word From the Lord

Some time ago just before a meeting in which I was teaching on this very subject, someone handed my husband a written word from the Lord and asked him to give it to me. I am sure that person had no idea what direction I would be taking in that meeting, but the message certainly fit in with it. It also fit in with a prophecy the Lord had given me earlier, which I will share with you later in this chapter.

Both of these messages are divinely anointed, so I urge you to read them carefully in order to discern and digest what the Lord is saying to us in these words. The first one begins:

> I want you to face the mountain
>> so that you can see,
> when the mountain is out of the way
>> all there is left is Me.

The Lord is always there. But sometimes the mountain seems to be bigger than He is. That is why I encourage you to speak to your mountain, but keep your eyes on the Lord.

What does God mean when He says that He wants us to face the mountain? He means that we are not to be afraid or intimidated by the size of the obstacle that confronts us in life.

You and I need to grow to the point that we have no fear of the enemy or his works. Don't be afraid of the devil or the problems he causes. Know that through the power of the Holy Spirit, you can face any mountain and remove it from your path.

We always try to avoid obstacles. We are constantly running away from the things that oppose us. When we do that, we are in reality running from the enemy, because he is the one who throws up those obstacles for that very purpose — to cause us to become afraid and give up.

That is why we are told in Ephesians 6:11-17 to put on the whole armor of God and to take up the shield of faith and the sword of the Spirit, which is the Word of God, with which we can resist the enemy who comes to attack us. But did you ever notice that there is no part of the armor to cover our backs. Do you know why? Because God didn't think we would need it; He never expects us to turn and run away.

You and I are not supposed to turn tail and run from the enemy. Instead, we are to **...be strong in the Lord, and in the power of his might** (Eph. 6:10 KJV). We are supposed to know and believe that greater is He Who is in us than he who is in the world. (1 John 4:4 KJV.)

Now I have to admit that sometimes when we don't know what to do, the temptation is to give up and run. Sometimes when the problem seems beyond us, the easiest thing to do is simply to throw up our hands and quit, hoping it will go away. We need to be strong in spirit. **The strong spirit of a man sustains him in bodily pain or trouble...**(Prov. 18:14). We may not know what the answer to our problem is, but we know the One Who has the answer.

We must remember that most of the time our friends do not have the answer we need. Too often people run to each other for answers instead of running to the Lord. When you have a problem, do you run to the phone or to the throne? God has a specific answer and solution for every situation you and I will face in this life. We need to learn to go to Him to receive the wisdom that we need. He has promised that He will give it to us. (James 1:5.) But not if we are into works. (James 1:6,7.)

Worry is a work, and so is reasoning.

Do you know why you and I are always trying to figure out everything? Because we want to be in control. We have an almost insatiable desire to *know*. But what we really need is to *believe*.

Do you remember what Jesus told those who asked Him what they had to do in order to be doing the works of God? He told them, "This is the work that God requires of you, that You believe." (John 6:29.)

It is hard for some of us simply to believe, because we are "workaholics" — we are addicted to worrying and reasoning. Worrying and reasoning are habits that we have to break with God's help. Every time we catch ourselves engaging in these activities, we have to remind ourselves to put our faith in God and not in our works. We have to remember that if we are worrying and reasoning, we are not receiving the grace of God. And if we are not receiving the grace of God, then we are not in obedience to God — which brings us to the last two parts of that word from the Lord.

Obedience to God

Only I can move the mountain,

only I can push it away,

only I can conquer the problems

that you face today.

Your only job is to believe,
   to listen to My voice,
and when you hear what I command,
   obedience is your choice.

This does not mean that there is nothing for us to do. It simply means that our first duty is to believe. Then when God speaks to us and tells us what to do, we continue in that spirit of obedience and faith by simply doing what God has said.

Leave the Outcome to God

We don't worry about the results; we just do what God says and leave the outcome to Him, confident that when we get to the finish line, everything is going to be all right, just as He promises:

But I will not make it too difficult
   for the victory is already Mine,
and I will fill you with My Spirit
   and through you My grace will shine.
Not when you are perfect,
   like you think you need to be,
but when your heart is willing
   to become more and more like Me.

Grace Is Letting God

Remember, I was handed that word before the message of this book came forth in that meeting. Look at the entire word of the Lord once again and let it bless you. Now here is a prophecy that the Lord gave me years ago:

Very few of My children really trust Me or depend on Me. I have mountains, endless mountains of grace stored up that I've never touched because I find very few who open their hearts through faith to receive My grace. Do you really want to know what grace is? Well, listen and I will give you a new and a different definition of the grace of God. Grace is you letting Me do what I want to do in this earth through you.

Grace is not us doing anything, it is us letting God do things through us. Grace requires us to be absolutely still mentally, trusting in the Lord rather than worrying or reasoning.

Do you want to have perfect peace of mind? You can have it, if you really believe in the grace of God.

As we have seen, grace is much more than unmerited favor, it is the power of God coming to a person who doesn't deserve it.

Grace is God doing us a favor, coming in with His power and might to accomplish in and through us what we don't deserve for Him to do. And all we can do is to be filled with gratitude and thanksgiving. In fact, I don't think we can be truly grateful and thankful until we fully understand the grace of God. Once we grasp the fact that *every* good thing we have comes to us by the goodness of God, what is there left for us but gratitude and thanksgiving?

It is hard to give credit to God when we think that we deserve whatever we receive from Him. It is hard not to give credit to God when we know that we do not deserve anything we receive from Him. It is also hard to worry when we know that it is not by worry but by grace that all our needs are supplied.

Grace Versus Worry

Do you know why grace keeps us from worrying? Because worry deals with the past, while grace (unmerited favor) deals with the present and the future.

For the most part, we worry about all the things that happened to us in the past, things that we can't change. We worry about our mistakes and failures that we think have caused things to be as they are today and have destroyed any chance we might have of a future.

We think about the foolish, wrong things we have said and done, and we think, "Oh, I wish I hadn't said that; I wish I hadn't done that." That's where grace comes in. We have got to learn to trust the grace of God to go back and fix those past mistakes and change our future destiny.

God says that He has mountains of grace stored up, but what do we do? We work and struggle and strive and figure and reason. Because we don't know what to do about the past, we fret about the present and fear the future. Instead of believing that when we get to tomorrow we will have the answers we need, we worry and reason, trying to figure what to do today to redeem the past and save the future.

Instead of worrying about yesterday and tomorrow, we should rest today, trusting the Lord to take care of our past, our present and our future.

God's Plan
Carries God's Grace

For we are God's [own] handiwork (His workmanship), recreated in Christ Jesus, [born anew] that we may do those good works which God predestined (planned beforehand) for us [taking paths which He prepared ahead of time], that we should walk in them [living the good life which He prearranged and made ready for us to live].

Ephesians 2:10

It is so hard for us to enjoy life if we don't have assurance about today, peace about yesterday and confidence about tomorrow. Why? Because as long as we live we will always have to face situations for which we don't have all the answers.

"Oh, but if we have enough faith, won't we get to the point where that's not the case?"

No, there will always be something going on in our life that we don't know how to handle; otherwise, we wouldn't need faith, we wouldn't have to trust God. The Lord will see to it that we are always dependent upon Him. Do you know how He will do that? By leading us into situations that are over our head. That is why although we may get worried, God never gets worried. Why not? Because He already knows exactly what He's going to do. He has got a plan, a path and a work all ready for us.

But although the Lord already has a plan for us to follow, a path for us to walk in and a work for us to do, He won't give us all the answers today that we will need tomorrow. With each new day comes the grace that we need to live that day and meet the challenges of it.

You may have heard the story about the young man who was in prison and about to be burned at the stake the next day for his faith in Christ. In the same cell there was an older, more experienced believer who knew more about the way of the Lord. As it began to get dark, the younger man struck a match to light a candle and, as he did so, he burned his finger. Letting out a cry of anguish and pain, he said to his companion, "How can I stand to be burned at the stake tomorrow if I can't stand to be burned on the finger tonight?"

The older man calmly replied, "Son, God didn't ask you to burn your finger, so there is no grace for that. But He is asking you to die for your faith, so when the time comes the grace will be there."

No matter what happens, God is still in control. He has a plan to handle everything that we will encounter in this life. And His grace is sufficient to meet all our needs. (2 Cor. 12:9 KJV.)

God Does Not Waste Grace

Let us then fearlessly and confidently and boldly draw near to the throne of grace (the throne of God's unmerited favor to us sinners), that we may receive mercy [for our failures] and find grace to help in good time for every need [appropriate help and well-timed help, coming just when we need it].

Hebrews 4:16

One of the things that we fail to understand about God's grace is that although He has mountains of it, He doesn't waste it.

God is not going to pour out His grace upon us a week ahead of time just so we can wallow in it. Do you know why? Because grace is power, and God is not careless with His divine, wonder-working power.

There is no reason why the Lord should give us today what we won't need until tomorrow, just so we can feel all warm and cozy and say, "No problem." We get God's grace, His power, when we need it and not before. That is why we have to have faith, and that is why we have to keep continually seeking God. That keeps us from feeling so secure in our natural self that we get to thinking we don't need God. Instead, we know that we have to keep the channel of faith open in order to receive God's grace to help in time of need.

One of the best things that ever happens to us is when we finally get enough experience in our Christian life and enough knowledge of ourselves that we quit having confidence in our own strength and ability. And that takes time to develop.

Another interesting point about grace, besides the fact that God does not waste it, is that it can be increased and decreased according to the need.

Sometimes special challenges arise in our life, things that are out of the ordinary pattern of our daily routine and which produce an unusual amount of pressure and stress. In such cases, we often discover that we have an extraordinary ability to bear up under those trying circumstances. In fact, there are times when situations develop which, by all rights, we ought to thoroughly despise, yet we find that because of the grace of God upon us we really don't mind them.

That kind of thing happens because God's grace has the ability to increase or decrease in order to fit our particular need.

Right now you may be finding yourself in desperate need of a richer, fuller measure of God's abiding grace. If so, call on the Lord and He will provide you all the grace you need to see you through that challenge to ultimate victory. Although God does not waste His grace, He is always ready to pour out upon us all the grace and power we need to see us through the most difficult of times.

Grace and a Bad Attitude

There are several things that can keep us from receiving the grace of God. As we have seen, one of these is ignorance, not knowing enough to call on the Lord, asking Him to pour out His grace in time of need. Another is a bad attitude.

Complaining and grace do not mix.

Many times the mistake we make is griping and fussing from daylight to dark, at the same time we are trying to activate the power of God in our life to help us solve a problem.

Many times the reason we are not able to tap into the grace of God is simply because our attitude is all wrong. You and I cannot expect God to intervene on our behalf in a situation if we are constantly grumbling, fault-finding, nit-picking and being jealous and envious. How do I know? Because that is the way I used to act. I had to learn the hard way that it just won't work.

There is also no way to receive God's grace while seeking sympathy from others or fellowshipping with self-pity. God will heal our wounds if we do not seek others to nurse them.

Many times we want the power of God to come upon us and solve some problem for us, but at the same time we want all of our friends to feel sorry for us.

If we are having money problems, for instance, we may go into our prayer closet and cry out to the Lord, "O Father, please help me. I'm in over my head financially, and I need Your help so bad. I'm trusting You to help me, because without You I have no hope. Lord, You are the only One Who can save me!"

Then as soon as prayer time is over, we go to lunch with our co-workers and spend the whole hour telling them all about how overworked and underpaid, unappreciated and underprivileged we are. We want God to help us, but we also want everybody else to feel sorry for us. It is not wrong to share your burdens in a balanced way and with right motives. But beware of seeking pity.

God never leads us where He cannot keep us. His grace is always sufficient for us — in any and every circumstance of life. There is no sense in our griping and complaining, worrying and finagling, constantly trying to figure out things, working ourselves up into a stew and getting all frustrated and confused. If we do, that shows that we have no faith at all in God's abiding grace.

If we want to receive the grace of God, we have got to learn to depend upon Him totally and not upon others' sympathy or our own self-pity.

Not Us, But God

Now let's consider the rest of the prophecy that the Lord gave me some time ago:

> Grace is you letting Me do what I want to in this earth through you. It requires you being absolutely still, unmovable, in your decision to wait upon Me to bring about the desired results. The ideas, the hopes, the dreams that are inside you are not yours. They originated in Me — that is, in My Spirit within you. It is not your job to bring them to pass; it is your job to be a vessel or a channel for My grace. No one of you can make anything happen that will be solid enough to stand up under pressure.

A Special Word

Please pay special attention to this part of the prophecy:

> This is the reason you experience so many ups and downs. You are trying to stand on the flimsiness of the flesh rather than the solidness of the rock.

The flesh is flimsy. It cannot be depended upon. The flesh will say, "Oh yes, I'll always be there for you," and then will go to sleep at the wrong time — just as the disciples did in the Garden of Gethsemane when Jesus asked them to watch with Him one hour. (Matt. 26:36-40.)

Are you standing on the flimsiness of the flesh or the solidness of the rock?

Not by Works, But by Grace

You do fair until the storm hits, and then you're right back where you started. You need to be emptied of human effort, the cares of daily living and fleshly frustrations. But you see, even this must be done by My grace. Effort cannot eradicate effort, frustration cannot get rid of frustration and care cannot eliminate care.

If you are like me, once you grasp this message about figuring, you will immediately set in to figure it all out. You will worry about the fact that it has been revealed to you that you worry all the time. You will try to reason why you reason so much.

That is why this word from the Lord is so "right on." Because in it He is saying to us that we cannot eradicate effort by effort, get rid of frustration by frustration or eliminate care by care. There is no way we can escape from dependence on *our works* — except by *His grace.*

Grace, Grace and More Grace

But grace can rid you of every hindrance. And you'll find as grace begins to flow, it will generate more grace and more grace and more grace and more and more and more until you've become that channel for My grace.

Once we learn how to receive grace, the result will be grace, grace and more grace all the time in our life. Do you know why? Because where sin abounds, grace does much more abound. (Rom. 5:20 KJV.)

You and I don't have a problem that is too big for the grace of God. If our problem gets bigger, God's grace gets bigger. If our problem multiplies, so that we go from one to two or three or more, the grace of God also multiplies so that we are able to handle them. It doesn't take any more faith to believe God for the answer to three problems than for the answer to two problems or even one problem. Either our God is big enough to handle whatever we face, or He's not. What is impossible with man is possible with God. (Luke 18:27.)

We can do *all* things through Christ Who strengthens us. (Phil. 4:13.) Trust me, if there is something that we are supposed to be doing, the Lord will give us the ability to do it. There is no way that He is going to lead us into a situation and then leave us there to face it alone in our own weak, human power. (Is. 41:10.)

A Never-Ending Flow of Power

There will be a never-ending flow of power, which is what grace is, that will flow through you, and the result will be that My desires, hopes and dreams and ideas will be birthed through you at no cost to you, with no carnal effort on your part. I will be glorified on this earth, and you will have the privilege and the honor of sharing it and being a joint-heir in that glory. My grace is available. "Come unto me, all ye that labour and are heavy laden, and I will give you rest." (Matt. 11:28 KJV.)

He that hath an ear, let him hear what the Spirit saith unto the churches (Rev. 3:6,13 KJV). I recommend that you re-read the prophecy and ask yourself, "Am I receiving the grace of God that is available to me?"

A Little Knowledge Is a Dangerous Thing

For I determined not to know any thing among you, save Jesus Christ, and him crucified.

1 Corinthians 2:2 KJV

This is such a glorious Scripture.

You and I try to know everything, and here Paul is telling us that he did just the opposite.

Unlike us, who worry about all the things we don't know, Paul was trying to get rid of some of the things he did know. Why? Because he had discovered that, as the Bible teaches, sometimes knowledge can be aggravating. (Eccl. 12:12). He had also discovered that knowledge can create pride: **...[Yet mere] knowledge causes people to be puffed up (to bear themselves loftily and be proud)...**(1 Cor. 8:1).

Sometimes the more knowledge we accumulate, the more problems we create. Often we plot and scheme and finagle to discover things that would be better left alone. Have you ever schemed to find out something that was going on and then when you did discover it, sincerely you wished you had stayed out of it? That is why Paul said that he had determined to know nothing but Jesus Christ, and Him crucified.

What Paul was referring to here is the fact that the natural man does not understand spiritual things: **But the natural man receiveth not the things of the Spirit of God: for they are foolishness unto him: neither can he know them, because they are spiritually discerned** (1 Cor. 2:14 KJV).

In my own life, what God impresses upon my heart does not always make sense to my head. The Lord has revealed to me that the reason is because my mind does not always understand my spirit. Sometimes the more I think I know, the harder it is to follow God.

The Mind of the Flesh Versus the Mind of the Spirit

Now the mind of the flesh [which is sense and reason without the Holy Spirit] is death [death that comprises all the miseries arising from sin, both here

and hereafter]. But the mind of the [Holy] Spirit is life
and [soul] peace [both now and forever].

Romans 8:6

According to this verse, this is not one mind, but two
minds. There is the mind of the flesh, and there is the mind
of the spirit.

That doesn't mean that you and I have two brains, it
simply means that we receive information from two
different sources. We get information from our natural
mind (which operates without the Holy Spirit), and we get
information from our spirit (through which the Holy Spirit
communicates directly to us).

We Have the Mind of Christ

For who has known or understood the mind (the
counsels and purposes) of the Lord so as to guide and
instruct Him and give Him knowledge? But we have
the mind of Christ (the Messiah) and do hold the
thoughts (feelings and purposes) of His heart.

1 Corinthians 2:16

Not too long ago someone asked me, "Just off the top of
your head, what do you think?" To be honest with you, that
is the way we live our lives most of the time — just off the
top of our head. But the Bible says that we are not to be led
by our carnal mind, but by the Holy Spirit Who indwells us.
(Rom. 8:14; Gal. 5:18.) The Holy Spirit can enlighten our
minds. When we get into what *The Amplified Bible* calls
"sense and reason without the Holy Spirit," then we are
treading on dangerous ground. The Holy Spirit is the only
One Who knows the mind of God.

This Scripture tells us that because the Holy Spirit lives
in us, you and I have the mind of Christ. The problem is
that although we have the mind of Christ and know the
Word of God, we don't listen to our spirit which is being

enlightened by the Holy Spirit. Instead, we listen to our natural mind, which relies strictly on sense and reason without the Holy Spirit.

In every situation of life, our head will be trying to give us information. It will be yelling at us so loudly that if we don't turn our attention to our spirit we will never hear what the Lord is saying to us in that situation. That is why we must learn to live out of our spirit and not out of our head.

Out of the Spirit, Not the Head

Early one morning as I got out of bed, immediately worry leaped into my mind. Today I don't even remember what it was all about, but at the moment it was disturbing and upsetting to me. That is the way the devil operates. He likes to attack us at our weakest moment, such as when we first get up and are still groggy, half-awake and incoherent.

That illustrates an important principle: *Satan never moves against strength; he only moves against weakness.*

As my mind began to revolve around and around that thought the devil had placed in my consciousness, the Lord spoke to me and said, "Joyce, live out of your spirit; don't live out of your head." That was such practical counsel that I have never forgotten it.

You see, evil spirits constantly bombard us with negative thoughts. If we receive them and dwell on them, they become ours because the Bible says that as we think in our heart, so are we. (Prov. 23:7 KJV.) If we accept the lies of the devil as reality, then they will become reality to us because of our "faith," our belief in them.

So after the Lord spoke to me and told me to live out of my spirit and not out of my head, I simply prayed, "Father, what do You have to say about this situation?"

By an impression in the inner man (which is the way God usually speaks to us), I immediately knew what He was saying to me about that situation:

"Joyce, you know you don't have to worry about that. How many times have we been through it before? Everything's going to work out okay."

"You're right, Lord," I answered. Then I went on about my business and never gave it another thought all day long. But if I had stayed in that mental realm, the situation would have gone from bad to worse.

That is why in moments of worry, stress and turmoil we have to simply take the time to turn to our inner man and say, "Lord, what do You have to say about this?" If we listen in faith, He will speak to us and reveal to us the truth of that situation.

Some time ago I heard a good report about someone else and all of a sudden I became intensely jealous. I share this story with you because I want you to know that no matter how spiritual you and I become, we are always going to be subject to such demonic attacks.

Immediately I reminded myself, "This isn't me. It is not my thought, and I am not going to receive it!" I was on the golf course, so I just stopped playing and took a moment to turn my attention to my inner man. I prayed and gave up that emotion of jealousy to the Lord. When I turned to the Lord, He assured me that I did not need to be jealous of anyone. He let me know that He has a good plan for my life also, just as He does for the person I had heard about. In a few minutes my jealousy was gone. If I had kept it in my mind, if I had nursed it and nurtured it, it would have grown and grown until it caused me all kinds of problems.

You and I have two huge vats of information within us. One is carnal information that comes off the top of our head. The other is spiritual information which wells up out of our heart. One is muddy, polluted water, and the other is clean drinking water. It is up to us to decide which source we are going to drink from.

Some people try to drink from both sources. That's what the Bible calls being double-minded. (James 1:8 KJV.) Do you know what it means to be double-minded? It means that your mind is trying to tell you one thing, and your spirit is trying to tell you just the opposite. Instead of saying, "I'm not going to believe that because it's a lie," you get in a cross-fire, going back and forth between the two thoughts.

If you and I are ever going to live the happy, victorious and successful Christian life the Lord wills for us, we are going to have to decide which fountain of information we are going to drink from. We are going to have to learn to live out of our spirit and not out of our head.

4
Supernatural Favor

4

Supernatural Favor

As we read the Bible from the Old Testament to the New Testament, we find several people who received favor. Let's look at some of them as examples for us today.

Joseph

> And Joseph's master took him and put him in the prison, a place where the state prisoners were confined; so he was there in the prison.
>
> But the Lord was with Joseph, and showed him mercy and lovingkindness and gave him *favor* in the sight of the warden of the prison.
>
> And the warden of the prison committed to Joseph's care all the prisoners who were in the prison; and whatsoever was done there, he was in charge of it.
>
> The prison warden paid no attention to anything that was in [Joseph's] charge, for the Lord was with him and made whatever he did to prosper.
>
> **Genesis 39:20-23**

Although Joseph was being punished unfairly because he was jailed for something he didn't do, the Lord was still with him and took care of him.

A person is really not in too bad a shape, even if he ends up in prison, if God gives him favor and places him in charge of everything that goes on there.

The lesson the Lord wants us to learn from this example and others we will be looking at is the fact that despite what happens to us in life, we can have favor with Him and with other people. (Luke 2:52.)

As children of God, favor is available to us. But like so many good things in life, just because something is available to us does not mean that we will ever partake of it. The Lord makes many things available to us that we never receive and enjoy because we never activate our faith in that area.

For example, if we go to a job interview confessing fear and failure, then we will almost be assured not to get the job. On the other hand, even if we apply for a job that we know we aren't fully qualified for, we can still go in confidence, believing that God will give us favor in that situation.

Many years ago when Dave and I were first married, we decided that I needed to go back to work for a while. So I applied for a job and was hired. I was very quickly promoted from one position to the next until I ended up being the equivalent of the second in command in the company. Although I didn't have the education or experience for that position, the Lord put me in it because His favor was upon me.

God wants to give you favor, just as He gave favor to Joseph, but in order to receive that favor, you must do what Joseph did and believe for it. Joseph maintained a good attitude in a bad situation. He had a "faith attitude," and God gave him favor. When God's favor is upon you, people like you for no particular reason, and they want to bless you.

Esther

Now when the turn for Esther the daughter of Abihail, the uncle of Mordecai who had taken her as his own daughter, had come to go in to the king, she required nothing but what Hegai the king's attendant,

the keeper of the women, suggested. And Esther won *favor* in the sight of all who saw her.

So Esther was taken to King Ahasuerus into his royal palace in the tenth month, the month of Tebeth, in the seventh year of his reign.

And the king loved Esther more than all the women, and she obtained *grace* and *favor* in his sight more than all the maidens, so that he set the royal crown on her head and made her queen instead of Vashti.

Esther 2:15-17

Do you know that there is a Scripture in the Bible that says that God brings one person down and lifts up another? (1 Sam. 2:7.) In this situation, He raised up Esther from obscurity to become the queen of the entire land. He gave her favor with everyone she met, including the king, because she had favor with Him.

Later on in the story, we recall that Esther drew upon that favor to save herself and her people the Jews from being murdered by the evil Haman who was out to destroy them. She was not afraid to go to the king and ask him to intervene on behalf of herself and her people, even though to do so could have cost her her very life, because she knew that she had favor with God.

If you find yourself in a situation in which you are being harassed, persecuted or discriminated against, if someone is trying to take something from you that rightfully belongs to you — whether it is your job, your home, your reputation or anything in life — don't try to retaliate by seeking natural favor. Instead, believe God for supernatural favor, because despite how hopeless things may look from a human perspective, God can lift up and He can bring down.

Every single day when you go to work, you should say, "I believe that I have favor in this place today. I believe that the light of the Lord shines upon me and that I have favor with everyone, with God and with man."

Don't go through life being afraid that nobody likes you. Don't harbor a fear of rejection. Instead, believe that God is causing everyone you come in contact with to like you, to want to be around you, to look upon you with favor.

Natural Favor Versus Supernatural Favor

Almost twenty years ago when I first started ministering, I was scared. I was afraid of being rejected. In those days, for a woman to do what I was doing was even less popular than it is today when women preachers are more widely accepted.

I knew that there were people, especially new people, who came to my meetings with a judgmental eye. I knew they were weighing and analyzing everything they saw and heard. So I bent over backward to speak and behave the way I thought they expected of me. I was overly cautious about everything I said and did because I wanted everyone to like me and accept me.

That is not normal. And it won't work. Trying to get favor on your own is not only hard work; it is often pointless. Usually the harder you try to please everyone, the more mistakes you make and the less people are attracted to you.

The problem was that I was trying to win natural favor. That is all I knew to do. Until about ten years ago I knew nothing about supernatural favor. I didn't know that favor is a part of grace. In fact, in the English New Testament the word *grace* and the word *favor* are both translated from the same Greek word *charis*.[1] So the grace of God is the favor of God. And the favor of God is the grace of God — that which

---

[1]James Strong, *Strong's Exhaustive Concordance of the Bible* (Nashville: Abingdon, 1890), "Greek Dictionary of the New Testament," p. 77, entry #5485.

causes things to happen in our life that need to happen, through the channel of our faith. It is the power of God coming through our faith to do what we cannot do on our own.

Favor, like grace, cannot be bought by faith, but faith is the channel through which we receive God's grace and favor and all of His many blessings.

Grace is the power to change us and to change our circumstances. It is not by human power, or by human might, but by the Holy Spirit that we receive favor. One of the twenty-five names of the Holy Spirit found in the Bible is "the Spirit of grace." It is by God's Spirit of grace that we find favor with God and with man.

So grace is the power of God coming to us through the channel of our faith, but in a very specific area. Favor is the acceptance and blessing that others show toward us because we have God's grace shining upon us. God shines His light on us. He draws attention to us.

Now although that light is real, it is usually invisible to the human eye. Most of the time people don't even know why they look upon us with favor. They don't know why they like us, accept us, trust us, approve of us, enjoy being around us, prefer us over others. They just do, because God shines His light of grace upon us and gives us favor.

When I found out about supernatural favor, I was just working myself to a frazzle trying to win the approval and acceptance of others. From that time on, I began to believe God for His supernatural favor, and it took the pressure off me. No longer did I have to worry about what kind of impression I was making on those who came to my meetings.

Now almost every single weekend I stand before a different group of people I have never seen before and minister to them. If I hadn't learned to believe the Lord for favor, I couldn't do that. The pressure would ruin my nerves. But now it doesn't bother me a bit.

Once you believe God for supernatural favor, it relieves the stress that builds up on you. Rather than trying to do everything for yourself, you are set free to truly enjoy what you are doing because you know that it is no longer your problem how the people choose to respond to you. You just do the best you can and leave the results to God.

You don't do as I used to do and try to gain acceptance by playing up to everyone you meet. You don't have to be phoney in order to impress people. You don't have to connive and manipulate and flatter, working and worrying day and night trying to say and do all the right things so you will be well thought of. Like me, you can give up all that because you are no longer seeking natural favor, but receiving supernatural favor.

The Difference Between Natural Favor and Supernatural Favor

There is an important difference between natural favor and supernatural favor. Natural favor can be earned, supernatural favor can't.

If you and I work at it hard enough and long enough, we can get people to like and accept us most of the time. But God doesn't want us to spend our time and energy trying to earn favor with Him or with others. He wants us to devote our time and energy to doing His will, whether it is popular or not.

Supernatural favor cannot be earned; it is a gift. That is the kind of favor God wants us to have, and the way we get it is simply by believing for it and receiving it from God.

One reason we are not to spend our time and energy seeking natural favor is because it is so fleeting. Here is a lesson the Lord would have us learn:

If you get acceptance with people by your own works, you must maintain it the same way you got it.

This is where so many people get into trouble. That is when they come under the power and influence of demons of manipulation and control. These spirits will work through people if we let them.

If you and I try to get people to like and accept us by saying and doing all the right things, we will have to keep on saying and doing all those things in order to keep their friendship and approval. And that is a form of bondage. We are no longer free to be led by God, but we must please the people or they might reject us.

But supernatural favor does not depend upon pleasing people all the time. It depends upon God's grace to give acceptance and maintain it. That is why I pray daily for favor, supernatural favor. I cannot tell you how many times I have seen God move supernaturally in my life and give me favor. He is getting me into areas in which to minister that, based on my own knowledge and ability, I have no business being. Sometimes it amazes me when I see the things God is allowing me to do and the places He is allowing me to go — not to mention all the precious people He is drawing to my meetings.

All I can do is say, "Thank You, Lord."

Whenever we quit trying to do it ourselves and start allowing the Lord to give us His favor, it creates within us a thankful and grateful heart.

When we struggle and strain and strive to get acceptance on our own, then we want to give credit to ourselves and our abilities and efforts. But when we know that everything we have and enjoy is a gift from God, a result of His supernatural favor upon us, then there is nothing left for us to do but say, "Thank You, Lord."

We are always more grateful for what we know we don't deserve than we are for what we think we do deserve. That is human nature. And that is one reason why the Lord resists the proud, but gives grace (unmerited, supernatural favor) to the humble. (James 4:6.)

Daniel and the Hebrew Children

In the third year of the reign of Jehoiakim king of Judah, Nebuchadnezzar king of Babylon came to Jerusalem and besieged it.

And the Lord gave Jehoiakim king of Judah into his hand, along with a part of the vessels of the house of God; and he carried them into the land of Shinar (Babylonia) to the house of his god and placed the vessels in the treasury of his god.

And the [Babylonian] king told Ashpenaz, the master of his eunuchs, to bring in some of the children of Israel, both of the royal family and of the nobility....

Among these were of the children of Judah: Daniel, Hananiah, Mishael, and Azariah.

The chief of the eunuchs gave them names: Daniel he called Belteshazzar [the king's attendant], Hananiah he called Shadrach, Mishael he called Meshach, and Azariah he called Abednego.

But Daniel determined in his heart that he would not defile himself by [eating his portion of] the king's rich and dainty food or by [drinking] the wine which he drank; therefore he requested of the chief of the eunuchs that he might [be allowed] not to defile himself.

Now God made Daniel to find favor, compassion, and loving-kindness with the chief of the eunuchs.

Daniel 1:1-3,6-9

In this passage we are reminded of a familiar story.

Because of their sins against the Lord, the nation of Judah was carried away into captivity in Babylon. There, some of the most promising of them, including Daniel and three of his friends, were chosen to become attendants to the Babylonian king. As part of their three-year period of training and preparation, these young men were supposed to follow a diet of rich meat and wine provided from the table of the king. However, Daniel and his friends determined that they would not defile themselves by eating the king's food and drinking his wine. Instead, they asked the eunuch in charge of their formation if it would be possible for them to follow their own diet of vegetables and water.

The Bible tells us that the Lord gave Daniel favor (compassion and loving-kindness) with the eunuch who agreed to allow them to follow their diet as long as it didn't harm them. Of course, not only did it not harm them, it made them stronger and healthier than all the other young men in training as royal attendants. In fact, the king was so impressed by them that he chose them out of all the young men to serve as his trusted counsellors. (vv. 10-20.)

The favor of the Lord rested on Daniel and his friends so strongly that eventually Daniel rose to become prime minister of Babylon, then the world's greatest power, and the other three were made high officials in the kingdom.

Do you think that would have happened if Daniel and the Hebrew children had tried to promote themselves by seeking natural favor?

Jesus

And Jesus increased in wisdom (in broad and full understanding) and in stature and years, and in favor with God and man.

Luke 2:52

From childhood, Jesus had extreme favor with God and men. In fact, once He began His public ministry, He was so popular with the people that He could hardly find time to get alone to pray and fellowship with His heavenly Father.

Even those who did not believe in Him recognized that He enjoyed favor with God and with men. When the Pharisees sent guards to arrest Jesus because He was claiming to be the Son of God, the guards went back empty-handed, saying, "Never have we heard anyone talk like this man!" (John 7:32,45,46.)

At the end of His life when He was brought before the religious and government officials of His day, Jesus had favor. Despite the jealousy and hatred of those who opposed and falsely accused Him, He found favor with Pilate, who would have set Him free had it not been for the demands of the multitudes.

Even as Jesus was being judged, Pilate's wife sent him a message saying, **...Have nothing to do with that just and upright Man...**(Matt. 27:19). She also recognized Jesus for Who He was, the Christ, the anointed — the favored — of God.

Pilate himself feared Jesus because he also recognized God's favor on Him. Otherwise why would such a powerful man try to excuse himself by washing his hands before a mob, publicly declaring, **...I am not guilty of nor responsible for this righteous Man's blood; see to it yourselves** (Matt. 27:24)?

After Jesus was crucified, the Roman centurion in charge of the crucifixion, **...having seen what had taken place, recognized God and thanked and praised Him, and said, Indeed, without question, this Man was upright (just and innocent)!** (Luke 23:47). The next verse says, **And**

all the throngs that had gathered to see this spectacle, when they saw what had taken place, returned to their homes, beating their breasts.

Why did these people react this way? Because they knew that divine favor rested upon the One they had just watched being crucified.

So Jesus found favor with God and men not only as He grew to manhood, but all through His life — and even after His death.

That is the way I would like for you and me to come to see ourselves, as the favored of the Lord. God sees us in a different light from the way we see ourselves. He doesn't see us as weak, helpless, sinful creatures. He sees us robed in righteousness, shod with the shoes of peace, wearing the full armor of God and wielding the sword of the Spirit, which is the Word of the Lord. That is how we ought to see ourselves.

The reason God sees us this way is because He looks at us not as we are in the physical realm, but as we are in the spiritual realm. That is how we must learn to look at ourselves.

Don't look in the mirror and say, "Oh, who would ever pay any attention to me? How can a nobody like me ever have friends, find a good job, get married, have a family or a ministry, or be a blessing to others? Nobody is ever going to want me."

When you do that, you are looking at things in the natural; you are not giving the Lord any credit for what He can do.

No matter how things may look to our physical eyes, no matter how we may appear to ourselves or to others, we must never forget that God can cause the light of His divine favor to shine upon us — just as He did for Jesus — so that we too increase in wisdom and stature, and in favor with God and man. (Luke 2:52 KJV.)

Ruth

So Naomi returned, and Ruth the Moabitess, her daughter-in-law, with her, who returned from the country of Moab. And they came to Bethlehem at the beginning of barley harvest.

Now Naomi had a kinsman of her husband's, a man of wealth, of the family of Elimelech, whose name was Boaz.

And Ruth the Moabitess said to Naomi, Let me go to the field and glean among the ears of grain after him in whose sight I shall find favor. Naomi said to her, Go, my daughter.

And [Ruth] went and gleaned in a field after the reapers; and she happened to stop at the part of the field belonging to Boaz, who was of the family of Elimelech....

Then Boaz said to Ruth, Listen, my daughter, do not go to glean in another field or leave this one, but stay here close by my maidens.

Watch which field they reap, and follow them. Have I not charged the young men not to molest you? And when you are thirsty, go to the vessels and drink what the young men have drawn.

Then she fell on her face, bowing to the ground and said to him, Why have I found *favor* in your eyes that you should notice me, when I am a foreigner?

Ruth 1:22-2:1-3,8-10

I am sure you remember the story of Ruth and her mother-in-law Naomi. After the death of their husbands in the land of Moab where they had gone to live during a famine, Naomi and Ruth returned to Judah. There, Ruth asked Naomi for permission to go out into the surrounding fields to glean grain for food so they would not starve to death.

While Ruth was gleaning, God gave her favor in the sight of the owner of the field, a man named Boaz who happened to be related to Naomi's husband. Boaz watched over Ruth, gave her food and water and instructed his harvesters not only to guard and protect her, but also to leave some extra grain behind for her to pick up. (Ruth 2:14-16.)

In fact, Ruth found such favor in the eyes of Boaz that he later asked her to marry him. As a result, she and Naomi were well taken care of for the rest of their lives.

That is a marvelous example and picture of the effects of God's favor upon a person. And that same favor is available to you and me if we will stop trying to get favor by works of our flesh, simply ask for supernatural favor and receive it by faith.

Definition of Grace and Favor

As we have seen, in Scripture the words *grace* and *favor* are both translated from the Greek word *charis.* We have said that grace is unearned, unmerited, undeserved favor and is the power that comes from God to help a person overcome his evil tendencies. We also saw that favor is the grace or power from God in a person that enables him to act graciously or favorably.

We saw that there is natural favor and there is supernatural favor. Natural favor is determined by how we treat people and involves things such as compliments, words of edification and human effort on our part to impress others. We should be good to people, but for the right reason. God's kind of love has no ulterior motive.

Natural favor can be earned, but, as we have seen, supernatural favor comes from God.

Although we cannot produce supernatural favor, because it is received as a gift from the Lord, it is true that as we do all the things that produce natural favor — being kind to others, treating people with respect and dignity, edifying and building up others — we are sowing seeds for a future harvest of supernatural favor. As we treat people right and look to God to give us favor, we are on the right track that leads to good, solid, godly relationships.

What It Means To Be Favored

It is often said of those who enjoy special favor with God or with men that they are "favored." To be favored is to be featured.

Each of us would like to be featured. Is that pride? No, not if that favored, featured position comes from God and not from our own personal ambitions or our own selfish efforts to call attention to ourselves.

To be totally honest, I find it delightful to watch God feature a person — especially if that person is me! I like to watch God move in my behalf, and I think everyone feels the same way. I must admit that it is fun to watch God single out someone for special attention and preferential treatment — especially in the presence of others.

This happens to all of us at one time or another, particularly those of us who expect it to happen and even ask God to cause it to happen.

For example, have you ever found yourself standing in a long line at the supermarket checkout counter in a real need to get through in a hurry? Have you ever prayed for God to help you get through quicker?

Sometimes in that situation I will pray and say to the Lord, "Father, please give me favor." Often another checker will suddenly come over to me and say, "Lady, I'll take you over here." Or perhaps someone in front of me in line with a cartful of groceries will pull out of the way and say, "Ma'am, you only have a few items, so go on ahead of me."

If this kind of thing happens to you, you have been receiving God's favor, perhaps without even being aware of it. Just think how much more it will happen now that you know to ask for it!

When such things happen, and you know it is a sign that you are being featured, that God's favor is upon you, then all there is left for you to do is say, "Thank You, Lord!"

God wants to give us supernatural favor because it provokes genuine praise and thanksgiving.

It is always enjoyable to have favor from God. It just seems that it doesn't happen as often as we would like. Part of the problem is us. We don't have nearly as much fun with the Lord as we should. We should have more freedom and liberty, and less fear and legalism. There are so many things that God would love to do for us, but He cannot because we won't ask. One reason we won't ask is because we don't feel worthy. The only time we will go to God and ask for special favor is when we are absolutely desperate, when we have gotten ourselves into a situation that we cannot possibly handle on our own.

The Lord wants to be personally involved in our lives. He wants to be involved with us in the grocery store checkout line. He wants to be involved with us when we get caught in a traffic jam and can't move.

When I find myself in that situation, I'll pray, "Lord, give me favor in this situation." Often He will cause someone else to open up and let me into the line of cars that is blocking my way.

In fact, that is a good example of how we can sow seeds of natural favor for a harvest of supernatural favor. When we let another driver in ahead of us, we are sowing the seed for God to cause someone else to do the same for us.

There is nothing wrong with being the featured subject, if we are willing to allow others to have the same opportunity to be featured by God also. To be favored or featured is to allow the Lord to shine His light upon us — for His glory. If we keep our attitude right, if we allow others the same privileges we enjoy, if we give God the glory instead of becoming proud and haughty, then He will continue to pour out His favor upon us and treat us like His favorite.

God's Favorite

What does it mean to be a favorite? It means to be particularly favored, esteemed and preferred. It means to enjoy special attention, personal affection and preferential treatment, even without being deserving of it.

If three equally qualified people apply for the same job but one is God's favorite, then the Lord will let His light shine upon that individual so that he or she is chosen for the position. Those making the choice may not even know why they prefer this particular candidate over the others; all they know is that for some reason this one has a special appeal to them.

There is nothing about you or me or anyone else that can cause us to become God's favorite. He chooses us for that place of honor and esteem by an act of His sovereign grace. All we can do is to receive His gracious gift in an attitude of thanksgiving and humility.

Now when I talk about being the favorite of God, I must make something clear. Because God is God of all His creation, and because He has a personal relationship with each one of His children, He can say to every single one of us at the same time, and sincerely mean it, "You are the apple of My eye; you are My favorite child."

It took a while for me to come to understand that truth. In fact, at first I was afraid to believe it. It was hard for me to imagine myself as God's favorite, even though that is what He was telling me I was. But then I began to realize that that is what He tells each of His children. He wants to say that to anyone who will believe it, accept it and walk in it.

Our heavenly Father wants His children to stand up and be everything that His Son Jesus gave His life that they might become. God doesn't want us walking around with our head down and our shoulders slumped, afraid to look others in the eye for fear of what they might think of us.

God assures each of us that we are His favorite child because He wants us to be secure in who we are in Christ Jesus so that we will have the confidence and assurance we need to walk victoriously through this life drawing others to share with us in His marvelous grace.

Crowned With Glory and Honor

O Lord, our Lord, how excellent (majestic and glorious) is Your name in all the earth! You have set Your glory on [or above] the heavens.

Out of the mouths of babes and unweaned infants You have established strength because of Your foes, that You might silence the enemy and the avenger.

When I view and consider Your heavens, the work of Your fingers, the moon and the stars, which You have ordained and established,

What is man that You are mindful of him, and the son of [earthborn] man that You care for him?

Yet You have made him but a little lower than God [or heavenly beings], and You have crowned him with glory and honor.

You made him to have dominion over the works of Your hands; You have put all things under his feet.
Psalm 8:1-6

Notice verse 5 which tells us that God has chosen man and crowned him with glory and honor.

In this context, the words *honor, glory* and *crowned* have special significance.

Here, in my opinion, *honor* and *favor* have the same meaning. We might say that God has crowned man with glory and favor, giving him dominion over the works of His hand, and placing all things under his feet. I describe the word *glory* in this instance as the excellencies of God. Of course, to be crowned symbolizes triumph or reward — usually in the form of an emblem encircling the head.

So what the psalmist is telling us in this passage is that you and I have been singled out by God Who has placed upon our heads His crown of favor and excellence.

Just because we don't see a crown on our head does not mean that there is none there. We don't see with our physical eyes the robes of righteousness in which we are dressed, but that doesn't mean that they don't exist in the spiritual realm. As the Apostle Paul tells us, the natural man cannot perceive the things of God because they are spiritually discerned. (1 Cor. 2:14 KJV.)

So you and I have been crowned with God's favor and excellence. The main reason we are not tapping into these blessings of the Lord which have been placed upon us is because we don't believe we deserve them or because we have not been taught they are ours. Our faith is not activated in this area. So we muddle through life, taking whatever the devil decides to throw at us without ever claiming what is rightfully ours.

If you will reread verse 6, you will see that all things have been placed under our feet by God Who has given us dominion over all His creation. That doesn't sound to me as if we are supposed to allow the devil and his demons to intimidate, dominate and oppress us.

We will walk in our God-given glory and honor only to the extent that we determine to do so.

Another way that I describe the word *glory* is that which makes something shine. A good Scripture to illustrate this point is Exodus 34:28-35 which tells how the face of Moses was resplendent after spending forty days and nights on the mountain with God. It was so bright that it frightened the Children of Israel so that Moses had to place a veil over his face whenever he talked with them after being in the presence of the Lord. I have also seen the word *honor* described as respectful regard, esteem, reputation, exalted fame.

If you and I will walk in the blessing of glory and honor with which the Lord our God has crowned us, not only will our faces shine forth with the glory of the Lord, but we ourselves will enjoy respect, esteem, a good reputation and fame — all of which are a result of God's favor.

A Personal Illustration of Walking in Favor

Once you and I begin to walk in favor, we will see fantastic things start to happen in our daily lives.

I have a personal experience to illustrate this point, but I hesitated to share it with you for fear of appearing haughty or prideful. However, after careful thought I have decided to include it in this discussion because it is such a good example of the blessings of the Lord that follow those who walk in His favor.

Some time ago a friend and I decided to take a shopping trip. I got up early that morning to spend some time with the Lord and had a wonderful visit with Him, enjoying His presence mightily for quite a while. As I came out of my house, I had no idea that there was anything different about me, but obviously there was because others reacted to it all that day.

When we spend time soaking up the presence of the Lord, no one can see it on us physically, but they can sense it spiritually. They may find themselves drawn to us without even knowing or understanding why. There just seems to be something about us that causes them to want to show us favor.

That is what I mean when I say that if we will walk in humility and obedience, God will cause His light to shine upon us and give us favor. There is a reward that goes with spending time in communion with our heavenly Father.

Usually I like to drive, but this particular morning I asked my friend to take over so I could spend some extra time with the Lord. So all through the forty-five-minute drive to the shopping mall, I sat there in the car reading the Bible and basking in the Lord's presence.

When we got out of the car and went into the mall, a lady came by and said to me, "Oh, Joyce, I know you; I come to your meetings sometimes." Then she added, "You look so beautiful! I can't get over how gorgeous you look!"

All I could do was say thank you and go on my way praising the Lord. And that was just the beginning.

Although it is common for people to recognize me and want to visit with me from time to time, I have never had such a day in all the years of my ministry. We were a long way from the place where we hold our meetings. But it seemed that everywhere we went, people went out of their way to greet and compliment me, telling me how good I looked, how young I appeared, how glowing I was. One woman in a shoe store even went so far as to tell me that I must have had a facelift because I looked even better than the last time she had seen me!

It got to the point that it was almost funny. But it didn't stop; it went on the entire time we were out shopping. I knew that God was responsible. I knew that all this was happening because the Lord was shining His spotlight upon me. I knew that it was nothing that I had done myself, but that, like Moses, it was because of the glory of the Lord that was upon me as a result of time spent in His presence. My face was shining and attracting others to me because it was reflecting His glory, not mine.

If that kind of thing has ever happened to you, if you have ever found yourself enjoying supernatural favor with people, it is because the light of the Lord was shining upon you. People may or may not have recognized that what they were seeing in you was God, but the result was the same.

When that happens to us, all we can do is to give God the thanks and praise.

Increasing Favor

I have given to them the glory and honor which You have given Me, that they may be one [even] as We are one.

John 17:22

We remember reading in Luke 2:52 that Jesus increased in favor with God and man. Now here in John 17:22 as He is praying to His Father just before His departure into heaven, Jesus says that He has given to us His disciples the same honor and glory that His Father had given to Him, so that we may be one as They are One.

That should be enough to get us all stirred up. There should be a lot of rejoicing going on after we have read that passage. We should be believing and confessing that we have favor with everyone we meet and in every situation we encounter in life. We should be praising and thanking God that His favor upon us is growing and increasing as we continue to commune with Him and with each other — walking together as one in humble obedience to His will, just as Jesus did.

Ambassadors for Christ

But all things are from God, Who through Jesus Christ reconciled us to Himself [received us into favor, brought us into harmony with Himself] and gave to us the ministry of reconciliation [that by word and deed we might aim to bring others into harmony with Him].

It was God [personally present] in Christ, reconciling and restoring the world to favor with Himself, not counting up and holding against [men] their trespasses [but cancelling them], and committing to us the message of reconciliation (of the restoration to favor).

So we are Christ's ambassadors, God making His appeal as it were through us. We [as Christ's personal representatives] beg you for His sake to lay hold of the divine favor [now offered you] and be reconciled to God.

2 Corinthians 5:18-20

Do you understand by this passage that God wants us — and through us, everyone on earth — to be in favor with

Him? Do you also understand from what we have said that the devil has stolen that favor through deceit and delusion? Jesus came to restore favor to God's people — and through us to everyone everywhere.

It is part of our *inheritance* to have and enjoy favor. It is part of our *ministry* to act as Christ's ambassadors by drawing others to receive God's wonderful gift of forgiveness and reconciliation and to share in His marvelous grace, His unmerited favor.

God wants to restore us to favor with Himself so that we may act as His ambassadors in the earth. That is how we need to look upon ourselves, as emissaries from a foreign land. The Bible says that we are aliens and strangers here, that this earth is not our home, that we are merely passing through. (1 Pet. 2:11.) Through us God is making His appeal to others to receive His forgiveness, grace and favor.

Now think about it for a moment: how are foreign ambassadors treated? Are they not treated royally? That is the way that we should expect to be treated, and that is the way that we should treat others to whom we are sent by the Lord for the sake of His Kingdom.

The Bible tells us that not only are we ambassadors for Christ, but that we are kings and priests unto our God. (Rev. 1:6 KJV.) That is why we need a different attitude toward ourselves and others. We need to be acting like royal ambassadors, like divine diplomats.

An Image of Favor

Put on God's whole armor [the armor of a heavy-armed soldier which God supplies], that you may be able successfully to stand up against [all] the strategies and the deceits of the devil.

For we are not wrestling with flesh and blood [contending only with physical opponents], but against

125

the despotisms, against the powers, against [the master spirits who are] the world rulers of this present darkness, against the spirit forces of wickedness in the heavenly (supernatural) sphere.

Ephesians 6:11,12

Lester Sumrall says that believers need to walk through life *militantly.* I often use the word *aggressively.* But we are both saying the same thing: we believers need to be confident and assured, not timid and doubtful. (2 Tim. 1:7.) We need to know who we are in Christ, fully persuaded that we have a right to be doing what we are doing.

Now I am not talking about having a bad attitude. I am not talking about being pushy or overbearing toward others. I teach a lot on humility and meekness and letting God open the door and make a way for us. I am not talking about how we treat other people, especially those who may not agree with us, I am talking about how we are to act toward the evil spirits who oppose and harass us. I am talking about behaving in the natural realm the way the Bible says we are in the spiritual realm.

We must remember that our warfare is not against flesh and blood, but against powerful spiritual enemies. If people have a bad attitude toward you, it may be because you are not walking in the grace and favor that God has bestowed upon you. It may be because you are abdicating your rightful position as a child of God. It may be because you are bowing down to demonic spirits, giving them the right and authority to frighten and intimidate you.

How Do You See Yourself?

And the Lord said to Moses,

Send men to explore and scout out [for yourselves] the land of Canaan, which I give to the Israelites. From each tribe of their fathers you shall send a man, every one a leader or head among them.

So Moses by the command of the Lord sent scouts from the Wilderness of Paran, all of them men who were heads of the Israelites....

And they returned from scouting out the land after forty days.

They came to Moses and Aaron and to all the Israelite congregation in the Wilderness of Paran at Kadesh, and brought them word, and showed them the land's fruit.

They told Moses, We came to the land which you sent us; surely it flows with milk and honey. This is its fruit.

But the people who dwell there are very strong, and the cities are fortified and very large; moreover, there we saw the sons of Anak [of great stature and courage]....

Caleb quieted the people before Moses, and said, Let us go up at once and possess it; we are well able to conquer it.

But his fellow scouts said, We are not able to go up against the people [of Canaan], for they are stronger than we are.

So they brought the Israelites an evil report of the land which they had scouted out, saying, The land through which we went to spy it out is a land which devours its inhabitants. And all the people we saw in it are men of great stature.

Numbers 13:1,2,25-28,30-32

When the Children of Israel drew near to their destination, the Lord instructed Moses to choose twelve men, one from each tribe, and send them on a scouting expedition into the land of Canaan.

When they returned, all twelve of them agreed that the land was fruitful and productive, that it was a land flowing with milk and honey. But when it came to deciding a course of action, ten of the twelve gave "an evil report," while only two of them, Joshua and Caleb, gave a good report. The reason the ten gave an evil report is because they were afraid. The problem was that they were looking at the situation in the natural, through the eyes of the flesh, while Caleb and Joshua were looking at it in the spiritual, through the eyes of the Lord.

Notice verse 33 of this passage in which the ten said of the inhabitants of the land and of themselves: **There we saw the Nephilim [or giants], the sons of Anak, who come from the giants; and we were in our own sight as grasshoppers, and so we were in their sight.**

How do you see yourself, as a grasshopper or as a mighty warrior of God? Is yours an evil report or a good report? When the Lord sets before you a new opportunity, do you fearfully moan, "I can't overcome the giants in the land," or do you boldly declare, "I'm going up right away, because I'm well able to take it!" Ten of the Israelites saw the giants...two saw God! Keep your eyes on God. You plus God is enough in any situation.

To be perfectly honest with you, I don't have the education or the natural qualifications of any kind to be doing what I am doing. I am the least likely person I know to stand before multitudes of people and preach and teach. The least likely to be on radio and television. I keep thinking, "Lord, how could You be doing this through me? Why do people keep coming back week after week to hear me speak? Why do they regularly tune in to our radio and television programs?"

In my ministry, I travel all over the country. Sometimes people I don't even know will come to my meetings and sit for two whole days just listening to me, hanging on my every word. Why do they do that? They do it because God is giving me favor. And He will give you favor too, if you are willing to receive it.

God can cause you to be accepted. He can put you over. He can give you the courage and the confidence you need to be a winner. But you have to be in agreement with His plan for your life. You have to quit seeing yourself as just the opposite of what He says you are. You must learn to change your self-image.

Not only must you learn to see yourself differently, but also to carry yourself differently. Don't hang your head when you are engaged in a conversation. I feel so sorry for some people. They come to talk to me, and they are so nervous and shaky they can hardly speak. Because I am someone who stands in authority, they seem to be afraid of me. That stems from a sense of insecurity. It is a sign of a lack of self-esteem.

When you talk to someone, stand tall and look that person straight in the eye. You have no reason to hang your head in shame or embarrassment. It doesn't matter how pitiful you may have been in the natural. Spiritually, Jesus died to lift you up and set you with Him in heavenly places. No matter how lowly you were before, you now have on your head a crown of glory and honor. No matter how you may have been dressed before, now you have on a robe of righteousness with a signet ring upon your finger. Do you know what that signet rings means? It means that you have authority. What you say, the Lord will back up.

Don't let the devil fill your head with thoughts of unworthiness. Remember: thoughts are seeds. Your spirit can only produce for you what you sow and nurture within your own mind and heart. Every thought you allow to enter and take root in your innermost being will begin to grow and produce fruit. That is why you need to learn to replace negative thoughts and words with positive ones. You need to stop seeing yourself as an unworthy sinner and begin to see yourself as the righteousness of God in Christ Jesus. (1 Cor. 1:30.)

Remember: you have as much right to God's favor as anyone else. Learn to avail yourself of it and walk in it.

Favor as God's Gift

...God selected (deliberately chose) what in the world is foolish to put the wise to shame, and what the world calls weak to put the strong to shame.

And God also selected (deliberately chose) what in the world is low-born and insignificant and branded and treated with contempt, even the things that are nothing, that He might depose and bring to nothing the things that are.

So that no mortal man should [have pretense for glorying and] boast in the presence of God.

1 Corinthians 1:27-29

One time while I was reading about Smith Wigglesworth and his great faith, I was tremendously impressed by all the wonderful things he did, like healing the sick and raising the dead. I thought, "Lord, I know I'm called, but I could never do anything like that."

Suddenly the Lord spoke to me and said, "Why not? Aren't you as big a mess as anybody else?"

You see, we have it backwards. We think God is looking for people who have "got it all together." But that is not true. The Bible says that God chooses the weak and foolish things of the world in order to confound the wise. He is looking for those who will humble themselves and allow Him to work His will and way through them.

If you and I will be careful not to get haughty or arrogant, the Lord can use us just as mightily as He used Smith Wigglesworth or any of the other great men and women of God. But the minute we get lifted up in pride, God will be obligated to bring us down. Remember: the Bible says that God can lift up, and He can bring down.

(1 Sam. 2:7.) The goal is to keep in mind that the power is not ours, it is His. He doesn't choose us because we are able, but simply because we are available. That too is part of God's grace and favor which He pours out upon us when He chooses us as Christ's personal ambassadors.

Christ's Personal Representatives

So we are Christ's ambassadors, God making His appeal as it were through us. We [as Christ's personal representatives] beg you for His sake to *lay hold of the divine favor* [now offered you] and be reconciled to God.

2 Corinthians 5:20

As we have already seen, we are Christ's ambassadors, personal representatives of the Son of the Living God.

That means that whatever we do, we need to do it with excellence. That means that wherever we go, we are to represent Jesus Christ to everyone we meet, to all we come in contact with. That is why we should always look, speak and act like royal ambassadors, regal emissaries. That is why we should take care of ourselves, our bodies and minds and spirits, as well as the things we own.

As Christ's representatives, our house and yard and car and clothes ought to be clean and neat and well kept. We ought to do the very best we can with what we have. That doesn't mean that we have to have the very best; we certainly don't have to have what everybody else has; but we do need to make sure that whatever we do have brings honor and glory to Christ.

Remember: it is through us, His personal representatives on this earth, that Jesus appeals to the world, begging them for His sake to lay hold of the divine favor offered them and be reconciled to God the Father.

What Paul is saying in this verse is that since you and I have received divine favor, our task, our calling, is to influence others to receive that same divine favor that the Lord wants to impart to them just as He did to us.

Shine On!

And the Lord said to Moses,

Say to Aaron and his sons, This is the way you shall bless the Israelites. Say to them,

The Lord bless you and watch, guard, and keep you;

The Lord make His face to shine upon and enlighten you and be gracious (kind, merciful, and *giving favor***) to you;**

The Lord lift up His [approving] countenance upon you and give you peace (tranquility of heart and life continually).

Numbers 6:22-26

Do you know what God's countenance is? It is His face, His appearance. When any man or woman of God says to us, **The Lord make his face shine upon thee, and be gracious unto thee: The Lord lift up his countenance upon thee, and give thee peace** (Num. 6:25,26 KJV), what he or she is saying is, "May others see God's glory shining upon you and through you."

May I encourage you to do something? As you leave the house to go through your day, ask the Lord to make His face shine upon you. Ask Him to lift up His countenance upon you and give you peace. Ask Him to shine His glory upon you, as He did with Moses. Then let that light so shine before others that they may see it and glorify your Father Who is in heaven. (Matt. 5:16 KJV.)

Letting your light shine can be as simple as putting a smile on your face. That is one way to "flip on the switch" of God's glory. The light of God's glory is in you, but if you never show it outwardly, people won't be blessed. It is amazing what will happen if you will just smile and be nice to people. Show favor as often as you can to as many as you can. By so doing, you will receive favor, because we are told that whatever we sow is what we will reap. (Gal. 6:7 KJV.) When we show favor to others, we receive favor from them in return.

Blessed To Be a Blessing

In closing this chapter I would like to encourage you to pray for supernatural favor. Pray for favor from all those you come in contact with. Wherever you go, pray that you will receive favor there. Also remember to pray for others to enjoy God's favor. God told Abraham He would bless Him and make him a blessing. (Gen. 12:2.)

Whenever I enter a restaurant, for example, I may pray, "Lord, I thank You that I have favor in this place. I ask You to bless me, and I bless all those in here." I usually receive better service, better food and better treatment. If you try this, and it doesn't work, don't get discouraged. The Bible says that there will be times when believers will be persecuted. We must keep every message in balance.

I will admit that there are times when I pray for favor in a certain place and am not treated well at all. But the vast majority of the time I see good results from practicing this message. I also believe that the way we behave during those times when we are not being treated well helps determine how much of this message we are going to see functioning in our life. When you find yourself in a situation in which things are not turning out as you would like, just pray and ask the Lord to help you stand the pressure, keep a good attitude and bring honor and glory to Him.

Everywhere you go, pray for divine favor upon all concerned — upon others and upon yourself. If you will do that, supernatural favor will rest upon you and you will be blessed to be a blessing.

5
An Attitude of Gratitude

5

An Attitude of Gratitude

I think we all know but need to be reminded on a regular basis that God desires a thankful people, not a murmuring, grumbling, fault-finding, complaining people.

It is interesting to note as we study the history of the nation of Israel that this kind of negative attitude was the major problem that caused them to wander in the wilderness for forty years before entering the Promised Land. We may call it by many names, but God called it unbelief.

God's attitude is that if His people really believe Him, then no matter what happens in life they will know that He is big enough to handle it and to make it work out for their good, if they will continue to have faith in Him. Joy and peace are found in believing, not in murmuring, grumbling, fault-finding, or complaining.

That is a lesson that we need to learn just as much as the Children of Israel needed to learn it. And one thing that will help us learn that lesson is a revelation of the grace of God.

Revelation Concerning the Grace of God

Now to a laborer, his wages are not counted as a favor or a gift, but as an obligation (something owed to him).

Romans 4:4

This verse implies that if a person works for his wages, then when payday comes around he is not really appreciative of what he receives because he feels that he deserves it since he has earned it.

This is a good example of what the Bible calls "works." (Rom. 4:2.) Works are the exact opposite of grace, which we have defined as unmerited favor poured out by God upon those who have not earned it and, in fact, do not deserve it.

There is nothing that can cause a person to become more haughty and proud than what he considers the rewards of his own works. And there is nothing that can cause a person to overflow with gratitude and thanksgiving more than a revelation of the grace of God that has been freely poured out upon him.

If you and I think that we deserve what we receive from God because we have earned it by our good works — our great amount of prayer, our daily Bible-reading, our regular tithing or sacrificial giving, our ability to operate in the fruit of the Spirit — then we are not going to be thankful and grateful. On the contrary, we are going to think that whatever blessing we receive from God is proof of our own personal holiness and righteousness. Then in turn, that proud, self-righteous attitude will cause us to look down on and judge others who don't seem to be as blessed as we are.

Too often we in the Body of Christ look at people who are having a hard time and think to ourselves, "If those people would just do what I'm doing, then they wouldn't be having all those problems." Although there may be an element of truth in that statement, we must remember what the Apostle Paul said about himself: "I am what I am by the grace of God." (1 Cor. 15:10.)

Let me give you a personal example of how we can develop a bad attitude if we take too much pride in our own abilities and accomplishments.

I used to have a real haughty, judgmental attitude toward anyone who had a weaker personality than I did. I looked down upon anyone who was not as determined to overcome as I was, anyone who couldn't handle physically, mentally and emotionally what I could handle. Finally, the Lord went out of His way to help me understand that, like Paul, all that I am is due, not to my great strength and power, but to His grace and mercy. He showed me that if He withdrew that grace and mercy for one moment, I could no longer be the person I thought I was and prided myself on being.

An Attitude of Gratitude

As I have shared with you several times, before God gave me a revelation of His grace, I was totally, miserably frustrated. Why? Because I didn't know how to allow God to help me with my problems. The breakthrough for me came as the Lord began to teach me about the present-day ministry of the Holy Spirit.

As I have already mentioned, one of the twenty-five names used to refer to the Holy Spirit in the Bible is the Spirit of grace and supplication. So when we talk about the Holy Spirit, we are talking about the Spirit of grace, which is God's power coming into our life to meet every evil tendency that we have and to help us solve every problem that we encounter.

We have said that every good thing that comes to us in this life comes by the grace of God. I believe that until we recognize that truth, we will never be the kind of thankful, grateful people God desires us to be.

As human beings, even we Christians are subject to selfishness and ingratitude. We can pray and believe God for something, and even be very thankful and grateful for it when we receive it. But it doesn't take us very long and we are no longer thankful and grateful for them, but actually come to expect them. We can even develop a demanding attitude in our relationship with the Lord. We can get to the place that we become upset and aggravated when the Lord doesn't "come across" with everything we think we are entitled to "as King's kids." As His children, we do have rights, and we have an inheritance, but a humble attitude is a "must." Without humility, we will be unappreciative and presumptuous.

As an example of how quickly and easily we can fall prey to a bad attitude, I like to use this illustration. We can believe God for a bigger house, and even be thankful and grateful when we first receive one. Then within a matter of months, we can find ourselves griping and complaining because now we have to clean that "big ole house!"

You and I have multitudinous opportunities to complain on a regular basis. But all complaining does is open the door for the enemy. It doesn't solve problems; it just creates a breeding ground for greater problems.

In this chapter I would like to encourage you to join with me in opening our hearts and allowing the Lord to teach us how to let the Holy Spirit, the Spirit of grace and supplication, come into our lives to help us in our everyday walk.

Let's learn to respond to the help we are already getting but don't deserve by developing an attitude of gratitude. This is not just an occasional word of thanks, but a continual lifestyle of thanksgiving. The person who has developed an "attitude of gratitude" is one who is thankful and grateful for every single thing that God is doing in his or her life day by day.

A Life of Thanksgiving

...Jesus lifted up His eyes and said, Father, I thank You that You have heard Me.

John 11:41

Here we see a good example of Jesus giving thanks to God. When you pray, I encourage you to end your prayer, as Jesus did here, by saying, "Father, I thank You that You have heard me."

One reason I encourage you to do that is because, as John tells us, when we know that God has heard us, we know that He has granted us our requests. (1 John 5:14,15.) The devil wants you and me to pray and then go off wondering whether God has heard us and is willing to grant us what we have asked. The way we overcome that doubt is by lifting up the voice of thanksgiving. (Ps. 26:7; Jonah 2:9.)

Part of the power of prayer is the power of thanksgiving because there is no powerful living apart from a life of thanksgiving.

During His earthly ministry, Jesus lived a life of thanksgiving. He gave thanks to the Father on many occasions and for many things. For example, He gave thanks to God for revealing truth to babies and hiding it from the wise and clever and learned. (Matt. 11:25.) He gave thanks to God when He broke the loaves and fishes and fed the four thousand. (Matt. 15:36.) He gave thanks to God when He took the five loaves and two fishes and fed the five thousand. (John 6:11.) And He gave thanks to God when He gave the bread and wine to His disciples at the Last Supper. (Mark 14:22,23.)

Now that we have seen some of the things for which Jesus gave thanks to God, let's look at some of what Paul has to say to us about thanksgiving.

Paul and the Lifestyle of Thanksgiving

Do not fret or have any anxiety about anything, but in every circumstance and in everything, by prayer

and petition (definite requests), with thanksgiving, continue to make your wants known to God.
Philippians 4:6

Here Paul tells us how to live free from worry and anxiety — by following a lifestyle of thanksgiving.

For many years I was taught (and believed, though I never bothered to search it out for myself or consult the Lord about it) that every time I asked God for anything, I should immediately begin to automatically and repetitiously thank Him that the thing I had asked for was on its way. I was told (and believed) that if I did that, then there was no way that the devil could keep me from receiving what I had requested from God in prayer. I was also told (and believed) that if I did not keep up a steady barrage of thanks for that blessing, I might not receive it.

Like many believers today, I was convinced that my being thankful for the thing I asked God for in prayer was the major force that would bring that blessing to me.

This Scripture may refer to being thankful for what we ask in prayer, and probably does. However, a few years ago God gave me a little different insight on it which I would like to share with you. What the Lord taught me is that when we come to Him in prayer, asking Him to meet our current need, He wants us to be thankful and grateful for what He has *already* done. He showed me that what He desires is not so much an *act* of thanksgiving, but an *attitude* of thanksgiving. He wants us to be continuously thanking Him for all the things that He has done in the past, is doing now and is going to do in the future. Then when we do come to Him with a need, it is simply one that we mention in the midst of our thanksgiving. I definitely believe our praise and thanksgiving should be more generous than our petitions.

Paul was speaking of this lifestyle when he wrote to us about **giving thanks always for all things unto God and** the Father in the name of our Lord Jesus Christ (Eph. 5:20 KJV). Also when he wrote to the Thessalonians: **Thank [God] in everything [no matter what the circumstances may be, be thankful and give thanks], for this is the will of God for you [who are] in Christ Jesus [the Revealer and Mediator of that will]** (1 Thess. 5:18).

This kind of lifestyle of thanksgiving is evidence of a grateful heart. The Lord revealed to me that if a person has a grateful heart for what he already has, it is an indication that that individual is mature enough to receive other blessings.

"But," the Lord pointed out to me, "if a person is always complaining about what he has now, why should I bother to give him anything else to crab and gripe about?"

The point is that in Philippians 4:6 Paul is not giving us a formula for getting what we want from God by constantly thanking Him for it. What he is presenting to us is a lifestyle of thanksgiving, an attitude of gratitude that gives thanks to God not only for what He does, but also simply for Who He is. Always remember this when presenting your petitions.

Paul's Thanksgiving List

And they yearn for you while they pray for you, because of the surpassing measure of God's grace (His favor and mercy and spiritual blessing which is shown forth) in you.

Now thanks be to God for His Gift, [precious] beyond telling [His indescribable, inexpressible, free Gift]!

2 Corinthians 9:14,15

Like Jesus, Paul thanked God for many things. He thanked Him that people received him as a minister. He thanked God for his partners. He thanked Him for the churches He founded. He thanked Him for the people in the churches. He even thanked God that he spoke in tongues. He especially thanked God, **...Who in Christ always leads us in triumph [as trophies of Christ's victory] and through us spreads and makes evident the fragrance of the knowledge of God everywhere** (2 Cor. 2:14).

But as we see in 2 Corinthians 9:15, the thing that Paul probably gave thanks to God for most, besides Christ Himself, was grace. Why is that? Because Paul knew that it is by God's grace that we receive every good thing that He chooses to bestow upon us.

You and I have all kinds of things to be thankful for in this life. The problem is that we get into the bad habit of taking them for granted. The reason we do that is because we never have to do without them. Because we are so used to having plenty of clean water and healthy food, good clothes and nice homes, convenient transportation and excellent education, freedom and safety and security and on and on, we forget that millions of people around the world do not enjoy these wonderful blessings. That is why I believe that if we are going to have an attitude of gratitude, we are going to have to do it on purpose. God will help us by teaching us and reminding us, but we will also need to develop new habits.

The Spirit of Grace and Supplication

The burden or oracle (the thing to be lifted up) of the word of the Lord concerning Israel: Thus says the Lord, Who stretches out the heavens and lays the foundation of the earth and forms the spirit of man within him:

Behold, I am about to make Jerusalem a cup or bowl of reeling to all the peoples round about, and in the siege against Jerusalem will there also be a siege against and upon Judah.

> And in that day I will make Jerusalem a burden-
> some stone for all peoples; all who lift it or burden
> themselves with it shall be sorely wounded. And all the
> nations of the earth shall come and gather together
> against it....
>
> In that day will the Lord guard and defend the
> inhabitants of Jerusalem, and he who is [spiritually]
> feeble and stumbles among them in that day [of
> persecution] shall become [strong and noble] like
> David; and the house of David [shall maintain its
> supremacy] like God, like the Angel of the Lord Who is
> before them.
>
> And it shall be in that day that I will make it My
> aim to destroy all the nations that come against
> Jerusalem.
>
> And I will pour out upon the house of David and
> upon the inhabitants of Jerusalem the Spirit of grace or
> unmerited favor and supplication....
>
> Zechariah 12:1-3,8-10

In this passage God is saying to His people that He is
going to destroy all their enemies and give them a great
victory by pouring out upon them His Spirit of grace (or
unmerited favor) and supplication.

There is no way to live in victory without an
understanding of the Spirit of grace and supplication.
These two words, *grace* and *supplication*, go together
because the Spirit of supplication is a Spirit of prayer, of
asking God for what we need rather than trying to make it
happen on our own.

So what God is telling us here is, "When the Spirit of
supplication comes upon you and you begin to pray in
faith, then My Spirit of grace will come flooding into your
life. Through that channel of prayer I will, by My power,
accomplish in your life what needs to be done, that which
you cannot do alone."

The people of the Old Testament never had this privilege. They had to work and struggle and strive and strain because they lived under the Law. And the rule was that if a person broke any part of the Law, he was guilty of the whole Law.

That is why the message of grace is such good news. It is the message of the power of God coming to us, free, just for believing it. Do you understand how wonderful it is that you and I don't have to be perfect in order to get God to help us? That we don't have to do everything just right, every day of our life, before God will intervene on our behalf? That all we have do is to ask Him and then to have faith that what we have asked, He will do — even though we fall far short of perfection? That all we have to do to receive the help we need is to come fearlessly, confidently and boldly to God's throne of grace.

God's Throne of Grace

For we do not have a High Priest Who is unable to understand and sympathize and have a shared feeling with our weaknesses and infirmities and liability to the assaults of temptation, but One Who has been tempted in every respect as we are, yet without sinning.

Let us then fearlessly and confidently and boldly draw near to the throne of grace (the throne of God's unmerited favor to us sinners), that we may receive mercy [for our failures] and find grace to help in good time for every need [appropriate help and well-timed help, coming just when we need it].

Hebrews 4:15,16

Isn't it wonderful that you and I don't have to live under the Law, constantly struggling, striving and straining to reach and maintain perfection without which we cannot feel assured that God will answer our prayers and be gracious to us? Isn't it great that we can come fearlessly and confidently and boldly to God's throne of grace (the throne of His unmerited favor to us) and receive mercy and grace to help us in our time of need?

I have availed myself of that marvelous privilege many times.

There have been several things that God has done that have changed my life radically. One of those things was baptizing me in the Holy Spirit. Another was giving me a revelation of several verses on asking and receiving which I discussed in the first chapter of this book and which I would like to refer to again briefly.

Asking God

What leads to strife (discord and feuds) and how do conflicts (quarrels and fightings) originate among you? Do they not arise from your sensual desires that are ever warring in your bodily members?

You are jealous and covet [what others have] and your desires go unfulfilled; [so] you become murderers. [To hate is to murder as far as your hearts are concerned.] You burn with envy and anger and are not able to obtain [the gratification, the contentment, and the happiness that you seek], so you fight and war. You do not have, because you do not ask.

James 4:1,2

What makes us miserable and unhappy? Why do we get frustrated? Why can't we get along with each other? Why are we always so upset and in constant turmoil? Why are we not walking in joy and peace? The answer is obvious. It is because our lives are not truly submitted to and controlled by the Spirit of grace and supplication.

We all know that we can be born again and baptized in the Holy Spirit and still be totally miserable. As we have seen, neither salvation nor the baptism in the Holy Ghost is a guarantee of victory. There are other things that we have to learn and apply in our life if we are to live victoriously. One of the most important of these things is total dependence upon the Lord.

The great revelation that I received from this passage in James was the fact that not only was I not asking the Lord for what I needed in my life, but that my whole relationship with Him was based upon doing. I had to learn to come to the Lord, like a little child, casting myself upon Him in total dependence instead of trying to be independent and work out things for myself.

Once I received this revelation about casting myself upon the Lord and asking Him for what I needed, I started to ask for absolutely everything I could lay my tongue to. Instead of struggling and straining, I was casting and asking. Nothing was too large or too small for me to cast upon the Lord and ask Him to handle for me.

If my husband Dave wanted to watch a football game on television and the kids and I wanted to watch a movie, instead of starting a war, I would go into another room and pray, "Lord, if You want us to watch this movie as a family, would You please change Dave's heart?" I trusted God to change Dave's heart if it was not right in His sight. If not, I was willing to accept that also.

The Bible promises us that whatever we try to accomplish on our own, God Himself will not permit to succeed. He will block us or oppose us — until we give in, humble ourselves and come to Him saying, "Father, I can't work out this situation; if You want it done, You will have to do it Yourself."

That is why I say that we must be *totally* dependent upon the Lord, not merely trying to use "casting and asking" as just another form of manipulation in order to get what we want out of either God or other people. That kind of manipulation, like any other work, only produces frustration. The only way to find real peace and joy in life is by truly casting *all* our cares upon the Lord, asking Him to work them out as He sees best — and then trusting Him to do so. Ask God for what you desire, but trust Him to give you what is best for all concerned.

The Gift of the Holy Spirit

The Spirit of grace and supplication is the Holy Spirit, Himself a gift from God received by simply asking in faith and trust.

> So I say to you, Ask and keep on asking and it shall be given you; seek and keep on seeking and you shall find; knock and keep on knocking and the door shall be opened to you.
>
> For everyone who asks and keeps on asking receives; and he who seeks and keeps on seeking finds; and to him who knocks and keeps on knocking, the door shall be opened.
>
> What father among you, if his son asks for a loaf of bread, will give him a stone; or if he asks for a fish, will instead of a fish give him a serpent?
>
> Or if he asks for an egg, will give him a scorpion?
>
> If you then, evil as you are, know how to give good gifts [gifts that are to their advantage] to your children, how much more will your heavenly Father give the Holy Spirit to those who ask and continue to ask Him!
>
> Luke 11:9-13

This passage says basically the same thing as Matthew 7:7-11:

> Keep on asking and it will be given you; keep on seeking and you will find; keep on knocking [reverently] and [the door] will be opened to you.

> For everyone who keeps on asking receives; and he who keeps on seeking finds; and to him who keeps on knocking, [the door] will be opened.
>
> Or what man is there of you, if his son asks him for a loaf of bread, will hand him a stone?
>
> Or if he asks for a fish, will hand him a serpent?
>
> If you then, evil as you are, know how to give good and advantageous gifts to your children, how much more will your Father Who is in heaven [perfect as He is] give good and advantageous things to those who keep on asking Him!

Both of these passages tell us to keep on asking, seeking and knocking, on a continual basis, day in and day out, seven days a week, fifty-two weeks a year, so we may keep receiving what we are in need of.

How many times do we stay awake all night long wrestling with our problems, losing sleep over them, instead of simply casting our cares upon the Lord and asking Him to meet our needs — then trusting Him to do so.

Remember James 4:2 (KJV), **...ye have not, because ye ask not.** But also consider John 16:24 (KJV), **...ask, and ye shall receive, that your joy may be full.**

How often do we *try* to get healed without asking God for healing? How often do we *try* to be prosperous without asking God for prosperity? And how often do we *try* to handle our own problems without asking God to work them out for us?

Our mistake is failing to ask and seek and knock, failing to trust God, our loving heavenly Father, to give us all the good things that we have asked of Him.

That is the basic message of these passages. However, there is one important difference in them. In Matthew 7:11

the Gospel writer has Jesus asking, "If you then, who are evil, know how to give good gifts to your children, how much more will your heavenly Father give *good gifts* to those who ask Him?" In Luke 11:13 the Gospel writer has Jesus asking, "If you then, who are evil, know how to give good gifts to your children, how much more will your heavenly Father give *the Holy Spirit* to those who ask Him?"

Often we use this Scripture as a basis for receiving the baptism of the Holy Ghost, and that is fine. But I think there is more to it than that. Notice that both passages say that if we who are evil know how to bless our children with good gifts, how much more will our heavenly Father Who is perfect be willing to bless His children with good things. The most important of those "good things" that God wants to give us is His own Holy Spirit.

The Gift of God, the Spirit of grace, is the One Who brings every other good gift into our life. That is what the Spirit is given to us for, to bring forth in our lives everything that we need.

It was this revelation that had such a tremendous impact on my life. Up to that time I had been trying so hard to make things happen and to meet my own needs, but then it became simple: if I needed something, all I had to do was *ask*.

So now if I need help, I ask. Instead of spending all my time and energy and effort trying to work out my problems in my limited knowledge and understanding, I simply ask the Lord to take care of them, trusting Him to work them out for the best according to His divine will and wisdom.

What I realized was that the Holy Spirit has a present-day ministry. That is what Jesus meant when He said to His disciples that it was better or more advantageous for them if He left them, because then the Holy Spirit, the Comforter, the Gift of God, would come to them and abide with them and in them.

Now let's look for a moment at this wonderful Gift called the Holy Spirit.

The Holy Spirit as a Person

And I will ask the Father, and He will give you another Comforter (Counselor, Helper, Intercessor, Advocate, Strengthener, and Standby), that He may remain with you forever —

The Spirit of Truth, Whom the world cannot receive (welcome, take to its heart), because it does not see Him or know and recognize Him. But you know and recognize Him, for He lives with you [constantly] and will be in you.

John 14:16,17

Before the Lord gave me this revelation of the present-day ministry of the Holy Spirit, I didn't really comprehend that the Holy Spirit is a Person. Of course, I knew that the Holy Spirit is often called the Third Person of the Trinity, but I always referred to the Spirit as "it." I would ask people, "Did you receive 'it?'" But I am happy to tell you that the Holy Spirit is much more than that.

The Holy Spirit is a gift from God bestowed upon us by His grace, requested by us in prayer, and received by us through the channel of faith. His multiple role as Comforter, Counselor, Helper, Intercessor, Advocate, Strengthener and Standby can be summarized by saying that His purpose is to get right in the middle of our lives and make them all work out for the glory of God.

If you don't know much about the Person of the Holy Spirit, I encourage you to start studying and finding out all you can about Him. Because the Holy Spirit is in you, with you, around you, all over you. He wants to be personally involved in your life. He has been given to you to accomplish a whole series of things in you, through you and for you.

The Holy Spirit as Sanctifier

Nevertheless, brethren, I have written the more boldly unto you in some sort, as putting you in mind, because of the grace that is given to me of God,

That I should be the minister of Jesus Christ to the Gentiles, ministering the gospel of God, that the offering up of the Gentiles might be acceptable, being sanctified by the Holy Ghost.

Romans 15:15,16 KJV

In the King James translation of John 14:2 Jesus told His disciples, "I am going to prepare a place for you." Later in that same chapter He told them that He would ask the Father to give them another Comforter to abide with them always. That Comforter, of course, is the Holy Spirit.

So just as Jesus has gone to prepare a place for us, I believe He has sent the Holy Spirit to get us ready for that place.

The Holy Spirit is the Sanctifier, the agent of sanctification in our life. If you study the subject of holiness, you will learn that there is no such thing as a person becoming holy apart from a great involvement with the Holy Spirit in his life. Why? Because the Holy Spirit is the power of God given to us to do in us and through us and for us and to us what we could never do on our own.

Before my revelation, I had never had much communication with the Holy Spirit. Now, I firmly believe that we should pray to the Father in the name of Jesus, but I also believe that we need to fellowship with the Holy Spirit along with the Father and the Son. It was through my fellowshipping with Him that I came to understand the role of the Holy Spirit as Helper.

The Holy Spirit as Helper

We have seen that the word *Comforter,* used to refer to the Holy Spirit, can be translated in many ways according to the many different roles or functions He plays in the life of the believer. One of these roles or functions is that of Helper.

Now, I had never thought of the Holy Spirit, the Third Person of the Godhead, as my personal Helper. I can assure you that I was a woman who needed a lot of help, but do you think I was asking for it? No, as I have said again and again, what I was doing was trying. Because of my pride, my stubbornness and determination to do everything for myself, I would not humble myself to ask the Lord to help me. I didn't know how to ask for help from God, especially in simple, everyday occurrences. Things like fixing my hair or getting the house ready for company.

I thought we believers could only call upon God for His help when we got into a situation that was far over our head. I thought that our heavenly Father was only interested in getting involved in our lives when we faced huge, desperate problems that would fit into His divine category.

I cannot tell you what it did for my personal relationship with the Lord when I began to discover and understand that God was interested in and concerned about every little, minute detail of my life. I can't describe what a shock it was for me to learn that He wanted to help me with everything in my life and that every time I got frustrated it was because I was not asking for His help.

We all know that at times there will be intercessors praying for us and asking the Lord to intervene in our situation because we aren't able or don't know enough to ask for ourselves. But there comes a time when we have to take responsibility for our own life. Why doesn't God just help us when He sees we need it? Because the Holy Spirit is a gentleman; He will not interfere in our personal business without an invitation. He does not knock down our door; instead, He waits to be asked to come in and take charge.

So the Lord had to teach me that He wanted to help me even with little everyday things like getting my hair fixed the way I wanted it.

One time, just before going to teach a Bible class, I got so frustrated with trying to get my hair to hold a curl that I was on the verge of hitting myself on the head with the brush. I mean I was upset!

Don't you know that Satan dearly loves that kind of thing? Don't you know the devil is just delighted to see a grown woman beat herself in the head with a hairbrush because she can't get her hair to go the way she wants it to? Don't you know the enemy is just thrilled to find a Christian who is too stubborn and egotistical to ask the Lord to get involved and help her?

In my ignorance and pride I was playing right into the hands of the devil. But this day, the Lord was determined that He was going to get His point across to me. So when all else failed, I finally gave up and in desperation prayed, "Lord, You said that we have not because we ask not, so I am asking You to help me get my hair fixed. In Jesus' name, make this hunk of hair curl, amen!"

Then I tried again. Same curling iron, same piece of hair, same operation. I put the hair back in the curler, turned it backward again, curled it, took it out — and there was this neat little curl!

Now you may think that story is a bit ridiculous, but it has a point. Sometimes we have to come to the place in our life where we realize that unless the Lord gets personally involved in our situation, nothing is going to happen. You may never get to the place of beating yourself in the head with a hairbrush (I hope not!), but you may get to the place where you are tempted to do something even sillier — or more dangerous! You may have to hit rock bottom before you will give up your pride and anger and stubbornness and ask the Lord to get involved in your life.

This story about my hair just illustrates how frustrated I was at that time in my life because I couldn't get anything to go right no matter how hard I tried. It didn't make any difference how much faith I confessed, I could not change my husband or my children or even myself. Through that simple little experience with my hair, I learned that my only hope of making any progress at all in my life was by asking God to help me. That is when I began to become aware of the presence of the Holy Spirit in me and with me as my Friend, my Counselor, Helper, Intercessor and Advocate, my Strengthener and Standby.

The Holy Spirit as Strengthener and Standby

This last word has a special meaning and application to us in our modern jet age. We are all aware of airline passengers who travel "standby," meaning that they stand by the airline ticket counter waiting to step up and claim a seat on the first available flight. The Lord used this scene to teach me about the Holy Spirit as our Standby, One Who stands by us at all times waiting for the first available opportunity to jump in and give us the help and strength we need — which is why He is also called our Helper, our Strengthener.

I have learned that one of the most spiritual prayers we can offer is the one-word prayer, "Help!" I can't tell you how many times a week I will stop and cry out to God, "Help me, Lord, strengthen me. I know You are here because the Bible promises me that You are always standing by me to help me and strengthen me in every situation of life."

If we are ever to have real victory, if we are ever to enjoy the abundant life that Christ died to provide for us, you and I have to learn the simple scriptural truth that we have not because we ask not. As long as we keep trying to do everything ourselves in our own way and in our own strength, we not only frustrate ourselves, we also frustrate the grace of the Holy Spirit, because it is a vital part of His ministry to help and strengthen those who serve the Lord. He is sent to minister grace to us.

I am convinced that much of our frustration in life comes because we are not receiving the help and strength that the Holy Spirit is constantly reaching out to give us. More and more I am learning to avoid frustration by availing myself of that ever-present Source of help and strength.

Sometimes when I am preaching and teaching day after day, night after night, I get so worn out I just have to pray, "Lord, help me, I need Your strength." There have been times when I have led seven meetings in four days. Often I get so tired that I have to remind myself that my help comes from the Lord and cry out to Him, claiming His promise that those who wait upon Him will renew their strength. (Ps. 121:2; Is. 40:31.) In such moments, I always receive the help and strength I need to finish the work that God has given me to do.

But standing by to provide help and strength is just one of the roles and functions of the Holy Spirit. Another is that of Teacher, Guide or Counselor.

The Holy Spirit as Counselor

But the Comforter (Counselor, Helper, Intercessor, Advocate, Strengthener, Standby), the Holy Spirit, Whom the Father will send in My name [in My place, to represent Me and act on My behalf], He will teach you all things. And He will cause you to recall (will remind you of, bring to your remembrance) everything I have told you.

John 14:26

How often do we frustrate ourselves trying to figure something out? How often do we run to someone else for counsel and advice only to become more frustrated because we realize that the other person doesn't know any more about the situation than we do?

Now, I am not saying that we should never seek counsel or advice from others, particularly those who are trained in this area. What I am saying is that we need to be led by the Holy Spirit, even in seeking counsel and advice from other people.

We believers must remember that the Holy Spirit is our Counselor. In my own life, I have learned that if I don't know how to do something or how to handle some situation, I simply say, "Holy Spirit, teach me, counsel me."

I will be honest with you. My husband Dave and I are just ordinary people who have no idea how to run a ministry like ours. Without the help of God we would have no hope of being able to do what we are doing. I can't tell you how often we say to the Lord, "Father, show us, teach us, counsel us, help us, strengthen us. Holy Spirit, this is

Your ministry, and we are giving You full charge of it. Lead it in the way it should go."

When you surrender a situation to the Lord, then leave it with Him. Don't go on trying to handle it in your own strength and wisdom. I can tell you from experience, it won't work. It will only lead to more misery and frustration. Trust the Lord totally. Let the Counselor, the Spirit of Truth, guide you into all truth. (John 16:13 KJV.) That is what He has been given to you to do.

The Spirit of Peace

Peace I leave with you; My [own] peace I now give and bequeath to you. Not as the world gives do I give to you. Do not let your hearts be troubled, neither let them be afraid. [Stop allowing yourselves to be agitated and disturbed; and do not permit yourselves to be fearful and intimidated and cowardly and unsettled.]

John 14:27

This verse follows immediately after the one in which Jesus tells the disciples that the Holy Spirit, Whom the Father will send in His name, will teach them all things and cause them to recall or bring to remembrance everything He has told them. This too is one of the roles and functions of the Holy Spirit in the life of the believer, part of His ministry on our behalf.

There is no way that you and I can live in peace in this world if we don't know how to receive on a continual basis the ministry of the Holy Spirit. Why? Because we will try to live by works rather than by grace. As Paul has taught us, these two, grace and works, have nothing to do with each other. If we want to live in peace, then we must put aside our works and rely totally upon God's grace. We must trust His Holy Spirit as our Counselor Who will lead us into all truth and bring all things to our remembrance, giving us holy recall.

Do you realize how much peace can be ours if we will just stop trying to figure out in advance everything we need to say and do in every situation we face in life?

If you are like me, you wear yourself out trying to prepare yourself for every situation you are likely to run into in the future. You try to plan and rehearse every word you are going to speak in every interview and conversation.

Jesus is telling us here that we don't have to do that. He is telling us to trust all that to the Holy Spirit Who will guide us and direct us. When we do have to make hard decisions or solve complicated problems or confront difficult people, He will decide the proper time and the best approach. He will give us the right words to say. (Matt. 10:19,20.) Until then, we don't need to bother ourselves with it.

If we will listen to what the Lord is telling us here in this passage, not only will we have more peace, but we will also enjoy more success. Because when we do have to speak, what comes out of our mouth will be spiritual wisdom from God and not something that we have come up with out of our own carnal mind.

But in order to enjoy that kind of peace and confidence, we have to learn to trust the Holy Spirit. And the way we learn to trust the Holy Spirit is by getting to know Him, which comes from fellowshipping with Him.

Fellowship With the Holy Spirit

However, I am telling you nothing but the truth when I say it is profitable (good, expedient, advantageous) for you that I go away. Because if I do not go away, the Comforter (Counselor, Helper, Advocate, Intercessor, Strengthener, Standby) will not come to you [into close fellowship with you]; but if I go

away, I will send Him to you [to be in close fellowship
with you].

John 16:7

Here, in the last verse that we will look at in our study
of the ministry of the Holy Spirit, Jesus tells us that the Holy
Spirit is given to us that we may have close fellowship with
Him and He with us.

Before we leave this subject, I would like to challenge
you to do two things. First, I encourage you to take *The
Amplified Bible* and intently study every one of the words in
John 16:7-11 describing the ministry of the Holy Spirit,
asking yourself, "Am I allowing the Holy Spirit to be my
personal Comforter, Counselor, Helper, Advocate,
Intercessor, Strengthener and Standby, or am I trying to be
all these things on my own? Am I depending upon God's
grace, or my efforts?"

Second, I encourage you to come into close fellowship
with the Holy Spirit. When you wake up in the morning, say,
"Good morning, Holy Spirit. I'm counting on You to see me
through this day. You know my needs and my weaknesses.
Lead, guide and direct me into all truth. Strengthen me in
everything I put my hand to. Help me to avoid and resist
temptation and to meet every challenge I face. Give me the
words to speak and show me the path that I am to walk in
this day, to the glory of God the Father, amen."

Then pray to the Lord, saying, "Father, I pray that I will
receive the ministry of Your Holy Spirit today, in all His
fullness. Whatever I need, I ask You to provide for me
through the presence and power of Your Spirit Who is with
me and lives in me. In Jesus' name I pray, amen."

Opening the Way for God To Move

Now to Him Who, by (in consequence of) the
[action of His] power that is at work within us, is able to

[carry out His purpose and] do superabundantly, far over and above all that we [dare] ask or think [infinitely beyond our highest prayers, desires, thoughts, hopes, or dreams] —

To Him be glory in the church and in Christ Jesus throughout all generations forever and ever. Amen (so be it).

Ephesians 3:20,21

This Scripture passage sums up the whole message that I am presenting to you in this book:

Although you and I have to do the asking, it is God's power that does the doing.

God is able to do much more than what we even know how to ask Him for. That is another reason why He gives us His Holy Spirit to be with us and to live in us and minister to us — so we will know what to ask.

I encourage you to open the channel for God to begin to move in your life, in a mighty and powerful way, by doing a whole lot more asking. Ask and ask and ask. Keep on asking, so that you may receive, and your joy may be full. (John 16:24.)

Let Him Ask

Consider it wholly joyful, my brethren, whenever you are enveloped in or encounter trials of any sort or fall into various temptations.

Be assured and understand that the trial and proving of your faith bring out endurance and steadfastness and patience.

But let endurance and steadfastness and patience have full play and do a thorough work, so that you may be [people] perfectly and fully developed [with no defects], lacking in nothing.

If any of you is deficient in wisdom, let him ask of the giving God [Who gives] to everyone liberally and ungrudgingly, without reproaching or faultfinding, and it will be given him.

Only it must be in faith that he asks with no wavering (no hesitating, no doubting). For the one who wavers (hesitates, doubts) is like the billowing surge out at sea that is blown hither and thither and tossed by the wind.

For truly, let not such a person imagine that he will receive anything [he asks for] from the Lord.

James 1:2-7

In this passage James talks about how we are to react to the various trials and temptations that we all encounter in life. He tells us that such things bring out our endurance and steadfastness and patience. He says that we are to let these things do a thorough work in us so that we will come through them stronger and better than we were before.

Then he tells us what to do if any one of us is deficient in wisdom, if any of us doesn't know what to do in the midst of trials and temptations. What does James say that such a person is to do? Stay up all night fretting and worrying? Run to friends and neighbors asking their advice?

No, James says, "Let him ask."

That is the first important point, that we are not to worry and fret or run to others, but rather to ask.

The second point is equally important: Who are we to ask? We ask "the giving God." His nature is to give. He gives without finding fault with us. I find this to be extremely good news.

And the third point is just as vital: How are we to ask? "In faith." Why are we to ask the giving God in faith?

163

Because **...without faith it is impossible to please and be satisfactory to Him. For whoever would come near to God must [necessarily] believe that God exists and that He is the rewarder of those who earnestly and diligently seek Him [out]** (Heb. 11:6).

The fourth point is to ask in faith without doubting. We should make up our minds what we believe and not be double-minded about it.

James tells us that God is a giving God Who gives to everyone liberally and ungrudgingly, without reproaching or fault-finding. That means that when we go to Him, asking Him for help, He doesn't withhold His help from us because we have made a mistake. The reason we don't receive is not because we don't deserve what we are asking for, but because we are not asking in faith, because we have lost our confidence or we are being double-minded.

According to James, God is what kind of a God?

A "giving God."

How does He give?

"Liberally and ungrudgingly."

To whom does He give?

"To everyone."

What is His attitude in giving?

"Without reproaching or faultfinding."

The *King James Version* of James 1:5 says: **If any of you lack wisdom, let him ask of God, that giveth to all men liberally, and upbraideth not; and it shall be given him**. The word *upbraid* means "to scold or criticize sharply."[1]

---

[1]*Webster's II New Riverside University Dictionary,* 3rd college ed., s.v. "upbraid."

So we could paraphrase this verse by saying: "If you are deficient in wisdom, ask of the giving God, Who gives to everyone liberally, without scolding or criticizing sharply for mistakes, because He wants to help you, even when you haven't done everything exactly right."

As we have seen, the vast majority of people will allow God to help them only when they think they deserve it. I know that is true because at one time in my life I was that way myself. For years and years I would let God help me only when I thought I had earned it, when I thought I had done enough good deeds to deserve His help. That kind of thinking doesn't produce an attitude of gratitude, an attitude of thanksgiving. Because if we think we deserve what we receive, then it is no longer a gift, but a reward or "payment for services rendered." The difference between receiving what we do not deserve and receiving what we do deserve is the difference between grace and works.

That is why God will never allow us to manifest total perfection in this life. Because if we did, we wouldn't be dependent upon Him any more. There would be no more need for His grace and mercy.

That doesn't mean that we shouldn't keep pressing toward the mark of perfection; it just means that we will never fully reach it until He returns to take us home to be with Him. You and I are always going to need God and His grace in our lives, and because of that we will always be giving Him thanks and praise.

Thanksgiving: Forerunner to a Life of Power

Through Him, therefore, let us constantly and at all times offer up to God a sacrifice of praise, which is the fruit of lips that thankfully acknowledge and confess and glorify His name.

Hebrews 13:15

Thanksgiving, gratitude and praise are forerunners to a life of power. Praise is "a tale" or a "narration," a telling of something that has gone on in a person's life. It is "the genuine confession of facts in one's life which gives glory to God.[2]

In other words, if we will continue to ask God, if we will keep receiving His grace and power, we will be so amazed that we will always have a tale to tell about the marvelous things He is doing for us — things that we don't deserve. Our mouths will become fountains of overflowing praise in recognition of the good things that the Lord is doing in our lives day by day.

As we see in Hebrews 13:15, we will be constantly and at all times offering up to God a sacrifice of praise, the fruit of our lips that thankfully acknowledge and confess and glorify His name.

To Him be honor and praise and glory, now and forever!

---

[2]W.E. Vine, *Vine's Expository Dictionary of Old and New Testament Words* (Old Tappan: Fleming H. Revell Company, 1981), Vol. 3: Lo-Ser, p. 198.

6
Living a Holy Life by Grace

6

Living a Holy Life by Grace

But by the grace of God I am what I am: and his
grace which was bestowed upon me was not in vain;
but I laboured more abundantly than they all: yet not I,
but the grace of God which was with me.

1 Corinthians 15:10 KJV

We have seen that in Galatians 2:21 (KJV) Paul said, **I do
not frustrate the grace of God....,** meaning that he did not
try to substitute his own works for the gift of God's grace.

Here in this verse Paul says that he is what he is, not by
his own efforts, but by God's grace, adding that that grace
was not bestowed upon him in vain.

The word *vain* means "useless" or "to no purpose." God
does not pour out His grace upon us for no reason or
without a real goal in mind. God's grace is bestowed upon
us not just so we can enjoy it, but so we can be empowered
to do something with it.

We have defined grace as undeserved favor. That is
one aspect of grace, probably the one that we are most
accustomed to hearing about, and it is wonderful. But
we have also seen that grace is much more than that.
Grace is power — the power of the Holy Spirit to come
into our life and overcome our own evil tendencies. If
that is true, then those of us who have received an
"abundance of grace" (Rom. 5:17 KJV) ought to be able to
live a holy life.

Be Holy

[Live] as children of obedience [to God]; do not conform yourselves to the evil desires [that governed you] in your former ignorance [when you did not know the requirements of the Gospel].

But as the One Who called you is holy, you yourselves also be holy in all your conduct and manner of living.

For it is written, You shall be holy, for I am holy.
1 Peter 1:14-16

It is obvious from this passage that God expects His children to be holy just as He is holy. This word *holy* is small in size but big in importance. To be so tiny, it says a lot.

What does it mean to be holy? What is holiness? Basically, *holiness* is "separation to God," a separation that should result in "conduct befitting those so separated."[1]

In the Word of God those of us who have put our faith in Jesus Christ as Savior and Lord are called *saints*, another word used to describe those who are holy. As saints, as holy ones, we are supposed to represent the Holy One Who has called us out of the world and separated us unto Himself for His design and purpose. (Rom. 8:28.)

Our Holy Helper

The Holy Spirit is called by that name for a reason. Sometimes we get so used to hearing that name that we forget what it is really saying. He is called holy because that is what He is, and His purpose in taking up residence in us is to make us holy too.

---

[1]W.E. Vine, *Vine's Expository Dictionary of Old and New Testament Words* (Old Tappan: Fleming H. Revell Company, 1981), Vol. 2: E-Li, p. 225

But while God wants and requires us to be holy, He realizes our weakness and inability. He knows that without help we can never be what He desires for us to be or do what He wants us to do. That is why He has sent His Spirit (the Comforter, Counselor, Helper, Intercessor, Advocate, Strengthener, and Standby) to help us to fulfill His design and purpose for us.

I have said that Jesus has gone to prepare a place for us, and that the Holy Spirit has been sent to prepare us for that place. That is not a Scripture, but it is scriptural; that is, it is a truth based on the Word of God. The process through which the Holy Spirit makes us holy, or leads us into holiness, is called sanctification.

Sanctification

Sanctification is a word that is found throughout the New Testament. It simply refers to the process that God uses to do a work in us by His indwelling Holy Spirit to make us more and more holy until finally we become just like His Son Jesus.

The finality of that process will never occur while we are in these earthly bodies. But you and I don't need to be concerned about that. The only thing we need to be concerned about is progress. The question we must ask ourselves is: are we making progress toward holiness, are we cooperating with the Holy Spirit and allowing Him to do what He wants to do in our life?

As believers we are not to be anxious about holiness or the process of sanctification, but we are to be serious about it. We are to recognize that it is God's will for us. We are to desire it with all our heart. We are to make every effort to cooperate with the Holy Spirit Who is working to bring it to pass in us day by day.

But while we are not to *worry* about holiness, we are also not to have a light attitude toward sin.

Grace Is Not a License To Sin

Moreover the law entered, that the offence might abound. But where sin abounded, grace did much more abound....

What then? shall we sin, because we are not under the law, but under grace? God forbid.

Know ye not, that to whom ye yield yourselves servants to obey, his servants ye are to whom ye obey; whether of sin unto death, or of obedience unto righteousness?

Romans 5:20; 6:15,16 KJV

When we talk about grace, we must be careful not to think of it as a blanket that covers us and gives us a license to sin.

When Paul started teaching the people of His day about the Law and grace and how the Law produces sin, but where sin abounds, grace abounds even more, the early believers got a bit confused. They reasoned, "Well, then, if the more we sin, the more grace abounds, and if God takes such delight in giving us His grace, then we ought to sin as much as we can so we can get more grace!" (Rom. 6:15.)

So Paul had to write to straighten them out, saying, "God forbid! Don't you know that when you sin you become a servant to sin? How can you go on living in sin when you have been declared dead to sin?" (Rom. 6:16.)

Like the believers in Paul's day, our problem is not just a misunderstanding of sin, it is also a misunderstanding of grace. When the Holy Spirit shows us what to do to keep from sinning and to walk in holiness, we immediately try to do it on our own without His help. We struggle and strive and strain, eventually ending up miserable and frustrated and confused because we don't understand why we keep failing.

That is why I preach and teach this message of grace, so that we can properly understand what grace is, why it was given to us and what it is supposed to accomplish in us — which is *to empower us to live a holy life*. I don't think we have finished a study on grace until we have learned that, that is to be the end result.

Grace To Live and Grace To Lift

If I have done my part in helping you learn to receive the grace of God, then both of us should see a practical, positive result in our lives. That result is that we get holier and holier and holier.

Grace is not just an excuse to stay the way we are, claiming that we don't have to do anything about ourselves and our lives because we are not under the Law but under grace. That is the mistake the early believers were making. That is why Paul had to rebuke them and correct their thinking.

Yes, God's grace will keep us from condemnation even though we sin. God's grace does keep our names written in the Lamb's Book of Life even though we aren't perfect. God's grace does save us, declare us righteous in His sight, assure us His blessings and a home in Heaven, carry us through this life and give us peace of mind and heart and many, many other wonderful things. But God's grace does more than all of that, it also teaches us to live as God intends for us to live — which is in holiness.

God's grace is given to us to do more than give us the power to live, it is also given to us to lift us out of sin.

It is dangerous to see only one side of an issue, because that leads to an unbalanced perspective. That is why some ministers won't preach on grace, because they are afraid that people will use it as an excuse to sin, to stay as they are and lead sloppy, undisciplined lives.

But I have a little different perspective on grace. I believe that if no one ever preaches and teaches grace, then believers will never be able to receive the power they need to rise above their sins and overcome their problems. I am convinced that most Christians are not looking for an excuse to sin, but for the power to live holy lives. If they can be shown how to do that, then they will cooperate wholeheartedly.

That is why I love to preach and teach about the ministry of the Holy Spirit Who is given to us to help us understand and live by the marvelous grace of God.

The Holy Spirit: Revealer of Truth and Empowerer of the Believer

Since by your obedience to the Truth through the [Holy] Spirit you have purified your hearts for the sincere affection of the brethren, [see that you] love one another fervently from a pure heart.

1 Peter 1:22

According to this verse, how do we obey the Truth?

Through the Holy Spirit.

How do we obey the Truth that the Holy Spirit, the Spirit of Truth, shows us?

Through His power.

As we have seen, part of the Holy Spirit's job is to reveal to us the Truth: **But when He, the Spirit of Truth (the**

174

Truth-giving Spirit) comes, He will guide you into all the Truth (the whole, full Truth)...(John 16:13).

The Holy Spirit is the One Who reveals to us the Word of God, convicting us of what we are doing wrong and showing us what we should be doing right. That is part of the process of sanctification. And once He shows us what we should stop doing and start doing, then we need to turn that word back to Him and depend upon Him to give us the power to accomplish it.

If I didn't know about the power of the Holy Spirit to help me do what He has revealed to me to do and not do, I would be overcome. I see the commands, such as the one we read in 1 Peter 1:14-16 about not conforming to the evil desires that governed us before when we were in ignorance and didn't know the requirements of the Gospel, and about being holy even as God is holy, and I realize my inability to do all that without help.

A message about holiness without a message about empowerment simply produces pressure. Because it causes people to go out and start trying to live a holy life without knowing how to do what they know they should be doing.

The key to the sanctification process is to know what is God's part and what is our part. That knowledge is revealed to us by the indwelling Holy Spirit, the Spirit of Truth, if we are willing to listen and learn.

Holiness Requires a Balance Between Rest and Effort

I appeal to you therefore, brethren, and beg of you in view of [all] the mercies of God, to make a decisive dedication of your bodies [presenting all your members and faculties] as a living sacrifice, holy (devoted,

**consecrated) and well pleasing to God, which is your
reasonable (rational, intelligent) service and spiritual
worship.**

Romans 12:1

Do you know what Paul is telling us in this verse? He is
saying that we are to dedicate to God everything about us
— not only our possessions, our money and time and
energy and efforts — but also our bodies, our heads and
hands and tongues — even our minds and emotions, our
attitudes.

If we really want to go to the extreme of holiness, then
our very facial expressions should be pleasing to God. That
means that when we are called upon to do something for
Him that we don't particularly want to do, not only are we
not to gripe and complain, we are not even to make an ugly
face. If we want the light of God's countenance to shine
upon us, then we are going to have to let our countenance
show forth His glory and praise.

We are to dedicate *all* of our members and faculties to
God as a living sacrifice, holy, devoted, consecrated
(sanctified) and pleasing to God, which is our reasonable,
rational, intelligent service and spiritual worship.

Often we get the impression that we are to serve and
worship God totally with our body and spirit, but here Paul
says that we are to serve and worship Him with our mind
also. We are not just to be physically and emotionally
dedicated to the Lord, we are to be rationally and
intellectually dedicated to Him as well.

This is part of the balance that comes when we dedicate
every member of our body — our head as well as our heart
— to God and His service.

The grace of God doesn't just fall upon us, we must
choose it. We have to make a rational, conscious choice to

follow holiness. God's part is to give us His grace and Spirit, our part is to give Him our mind and will.

If we become either too active or too passive, then we have a problem. There is a delicate balance to be maintained between rest and effort, just as there is between casting our care upon God and casting our responsibility upon Him. There is a real balance involved in distinguishing between resting in the Lord and being passive about the things of God.

In almost every scriptural doctrine, the reason people become confused and experience failure and frustration is because they get off balance one way or the other. Some people are like a pendulum. They swing all the way to one side. Then when they see that they are out of balance, they swing all the way to the opposite side, which is just as bad. They never seem to be able to find the center line between any two extremes. When the Spirit reveals to them that they are trying to do everything for themselves without depending enough upon Him, they react all out of proportion. They go from being totally independent to being totally dependent. They quit doing anything for themselves at all, thinking that God is going to do everything for them without any effort whatsoever on their part. Where they used to think, "I've got to do it all," now their attitude is, "If God wants it done, He will take care of it." God wants us to cast our care, but not our responsibility.

"I am casting my care on God" is a good confession if it is backed up by prayer and faith, which is our responsibility, not God's.

If you and I want to stay in balance, then we are going to have to stay in close fellowship with the Spirit of Truth. True holiness is a combined effort between us and the Holy Spirit. It requires a clear understanding of His part and our part, and a delicate balance between the two. Many believers keep the care and cast the responsibility. This is wrong! Cast the care, and enter God's rest, but be ever ready to fulfill your responsibilities empowered by the Spirit of grace.

The Nature of Holiness

Thus says the Lord of hosts: Ask now the priests to decide this question of law:

If one carries in the skirt of his garment flesh that is holy [because it has been offered in sacrifice to God], and with his skirt or the flaps of his garment he touches bread, or pottage, or wine, or oil, or any kind of food, does what he touches become holy [dedicated to God's service exclusively]? And the priests answered, No! [Holiness is not infectious.]

Then said Haggai, If one who is [ceremonially] unclean because he has come in contact with a dead body should touch any of these articles of food, shall it be [ceremonially] unclean? And the priests answered, It shall be unclean. [Unholiness is infectious.]

Haggai 2:11-13

We have defined *holiness* as "separation to God," a separation that should result in "conduct befitting those so separated."[2] In the New Testament, the same Greek word translated *holiness* is also translated *sanctification*, which the Greek dictionary says "cannot be transferred or imputed."[3] That means that holiness is an individual possession, one that is built up little by little. It cannot be given to or taken from another person.

In other words, you and I cannot become holy by going through a prayer line or by having hands laid on us or by associating with someone else who is holy.

---

[2]*Ibid.*
[3]*Ibid.*, Vol. 3: Lo-Ser, p. 317.

As we see in this passage from the Old Testament prophet Haggai, unholiness is infectious, holiness is not. What that means is that you and I can associate with someone who is living a sinful life, and that individual's sinfulness can rub off on us. We can catch it like a disease. But holiness is not like that. It can't be picked up by contact or exposure; it has to be chosen on purpose.

Holiness Is Individual

As for the man who is a weak believer, welcome him [into your fellowship], but not to criticize his opinions or pass judgment on his scruples or perplex him with discussions.

One [man's faith permits him to] believe he may eat anything, while a weaker one [limits his] eating to vegetables.

Let not him who eats look down on or despise him who abstains, and let not him who abstains criticize and pass judgment on him who eats; for God has accepted and welcomed him.

Who are you to pass judgment on and censure another's household servant? It is before his own master that he stands or falls. And he shall stand and be upheld, for the Master (the Lord) is mighty to support him and make him stand.

Romans 14:1-4

In addition to the problem of misunderstanding sin and grace, another major reason why people fail to live a holy life is because they try to live by somebody else's convictions about holiness.

As we have seen, holiness is an individual matter. Naturally, there are certain things that we know are wrong for all of us. If you are not yet sure what these things are, read your Bible and you will quickly discover them. But there are many other things that God deals with us about personally and individually. There are some that He even deals with us about in different ways at different times in our life.

One of the worst mistakes we can make is to try to do what others are doing or telling us to do just because they believe it is God's will for them.

Another mistake we make is very similar to this one. We also try to make others do what we are doing just because God has convicted us that it is His will for us. Both of these are big, big mistakes.

I must admit that I have a great weakness in this area — not so much in letting others influence me into doing what they are doing, but in trying to get others to do what I believe they should do.

As I mentioned earlier, I spent many frustrating years trying to change myself. I finally learned to receive God's grace (His power) to change me. I had to learn the same lesson about other people. I tried to change Dave and my children. I thought I knew what was right according to the Word, and I spent much time trying to convince them of the changes that I felt were needed in their personalities, actions and choices.

My "works of the flesh" only made the problem worse. My lack of acceptance of them as they were hurt our personal relationships, and they felt rejected and criticized. Only God can change a human heart. We can lay down rules and laws for people, but it drives them away from us. As we learn to wait on God, He changes all of us, and our change in behavior comes from a heart of "want to" — not "have to."

As a teacher, I have a certain ability to persuade people. That is a gift of teaching that flows through me. I have an anointing from God to take His Word and convince others that they ought to accept it and apply it to their lives. But this is an area in which I have to be very, very careful. I must be cautious not to go too far and begin to put my own personal ideas and opinions off on others.

When I first started out in the ministry, I was bad about that. I tried to cram my beliefs down everybody else's throat. Every time I had any success at anything, I tried to get everyone to experience the same success by pressuring them to do exactly what I was doing. One little victory in my life and I was right out there giving victory lessons!

Be careful about that sort of thing. Be on your guard against either letting other people put their convictions off on you or about putting your convictions off on them. The Bible says that we are to be led by the prompting of the Holy Spirit, and the Holy Spirit is given to each of us individually for that very purpose.

The problem is that so many believers can't or won't content themselves with hearing and following the Holy Spirit for themselves — and then allowing others the same right and privilege. They think that everybody in the Body of Christ has got to be doing the same thing the same way at the same time for the same reason. To them, anybody who doesn't fit the pattern is dead wrong and out of the will of God. By adopting this attitude, they fall into the trap Paul warns us about here of passing judgment on someone else's servant.

Our problem is that we are constantly trying to straighten out everybody else instead of setting our own house in order. It has taken me nearly a half century to discover this truth: we need to mind our own business!

Holiness is an individual matter. God deals with each of us in His own way and in His own time. We are all at

different stages of sanctification, which is a process that is
worked out by the Holy Spirit in a unique way in each
individual believer. It will hinder our own progress if we
become more involved in someone else's sanctification
process than we are in our own. We must be careful not to
become so concerned with what others are doing or not
doing that we fail to listen to the voice of the Holy Spirit
Who is dealing with us about our own life. We must learn to
take care of our own affairs and leave the criticizing and
judging of others to God.

Judge Not

Why do you criticize and pass judgment on your
brother? Or you, why do you look down upon or
despise your brother? For we shall all stand before the
judgment seat of God.

For it is written, As I live, says the Lord, every knee
shall bow to Me, and every tongue shall confess to God
[acknowledge Him to His honor and to His praise].

And so each of us shall give an account of himself
[give an answer in reference to judgment] to God.

Then let us no more criticize and blame and pass
judgment on one another, but rather decide and
endeavor never to put a stumbling block or an obstacle
or a hindrance in the way of a brother.

Romans 14:10-13

When I stand before the judgment seat of God, He is not
going to ask me about you, just as He is not going to ask
you about me when you appear before Him. God is not
going to hold me accountable for anybody else on earth
other than Joyce Meyer.

I don't know how much time I have left to work with
God to get myself straightened out, but I do want to be able
to answer the questions He asks me about me. If I stand
before Him and He says, "Joyce, why didn't you pay

attention to Me when I was dealing with you about your faults?" I don't want to have to answer, "Well, Lord, I didn't have time because I was too busy working to get my husband Dave straightened out."

According to this passage, each of us is going to give an account of our own self to God the Father. That is why we need to learn to work on our own sanctification and quit putting stumbling blocks, obstacles and hindrances in the way of our brothers and sisters in Christ. We will never all believe exactly alike on everything; that is why we are told to follow our own convictions — and let everyone else do the same.

Keep It to Yourself!

Your personal convictions [on such matters] — exercise [them] as in God's presence, keeping them to yourself [striving only to know the truth and obey His will]. Blessed (happy, to be envied) is he who has no reason to judge himself for what he approves [who does not convict himself by what he chooses to do].

But the man who has doubts (misgivings, an uneasy conscience) about eating, and then eats [perhaps because of you], stands condemned [before God], because he is not true to his convictions and he does not act from faith. For whatever does not originate and proceed from faith is sin [whatever is done without a conviction of its approval by God is sinful].

Romans 14:22,23

It couldn't be stated any clearer than this:

Keep your personal convictions (in this case, your ideas and opinions based on what God told you to do in a specific situation) *to yourself. Don't go around trying to put them off on everybody else.*

All too often we seem to have the idea, "God told me not to drink caffeine, so now the whole world has got to stop drinking caffeine! The Lord told me I can't have sugar, so it is my job to inform everybody on earth it is God's will that they stop using sugar!"

I used to have that attitude. Every time I got hold of a new insight from the Lord, immediately I got up on my soapbox and began to broadcast it to the whole world. If I was taking a certain vitamin, then everybody had to take it. Because if it was what God told me to do, then it must be what He had told them to do too.

That is what I mean when I talk about trying to cram our convictions down everybody else's throat. That is *not* our job.

Sometimes we try to excuse ourselves or justify our actions by saying, "Well, I'm just trying to help." We need to remember that it is not us, but it is the Holy Spirit Who is the Helper.

In my own life and ministry, whenever I have an impulse to help someone, I back off and pray, "Lord, is this Your desire, or is it just me wanting to 'do my thing'?" If I will wait a while, I will become settled in my mind and heart about whether what I am about to do is God's idea or mine.

Now, I am not saying that we should never tell anybody anything or that we should never offer to help those in need. I am simply saying that we have to be sure of our true motivation. Is it really to glorify God and uplift others, or is it just to exalt ourselves by making them over into our image and likeness? Are we really trying to help them, or are we just being bossy? Is it fleshly pride or God's grace that is operating?

In Romans 12:3 Paul said, **...by the grace (unmerited favor of God) given to me I warn everyone among you not**

to estimate and think of himself more highly than he ought [not to have an exaggerated opinion of his own importance].... Paul was warning the Romans, or we might say, correcting them, but he was humble enough to know that he had to do so by God's grace — not by fleshly zeal.

Verse 23 in Romans 14 tells us that the person who does something against his conscience (perhaps because of *us!*) stands condemned before God. Why? Because he is not acting in faith, he is not being true to his personal convictions. And whatever is not of faith is sin. That is, whatever is done without a personal, inner conviction of its approval by God is sinful.

This is all the more reason why we must be constantly on our guard against trying to put our convictions off on someone else. Instead of leading him to faith, we may be doing just the opposite; we may be causing him to sin because he is trying to operate off of our personal convictions rather than his own God-approved convictions.

Sanctification as a Process

And all of us, as with unveiled face, [because we] continued to behold [in the Word of God] as in a mirror the glory of the Lord, are constantly being transfigured into His very own image in ever increasing splendor and from one degree of glory to another; [for this comes] from the Lord [Who is] the Spirit.

2 Corinthians 3:18

Here the Apostle Paul says that as we get into the Word of God we are transformed into His image, going from glory to glory. That means that we have not yet arrived at the full state of holiness. We are more glorious than we were when we started, and we are getting more and more glorious as we continue to move forward toward holiness step by step, but we still have a way to go yet. Legally and positionally, we are Holy in Christ. But experientially, the holiness is being manifested through us in degrees of glory that are progressive.

That is what we have called the *process* of sanctification. Part of that sanctification process is "the separation of the believer from the world."[4] We need to ponder that statement every once in a while. As believers, we are to be in the world, but not of the world.

Although we are to pursue holiness "earnestly and undeviatingly," although we are to desire it fully and cooperate in it, holiness, "or sanctification, is not an attainment, it is the state into which God, in grace, calls sinful men."[5]

In Deuteronomy 7:22 God told the Children of Israel that He would deliver them from their enemies "little by little." In the same way, we are not delivered out of our sins instantly and effortlessly, without going through a process.

We want to move from sinfulness to holiness all at once. But God says that we must proceed step by step. Each step to holiness has to be made along the path of grace, which in this case is the power of God to continue to take the next step. If we try to go forward on our own effort, without depending on God's grace, we will fail because without grace we will become frustrated and backslide.

There is no way to travel from the state of sinfulness to the state of holiness except by the highway of grace.

Sanctification as a Seed

Therefore, my dear ones, as you have always obeyed [my suggestions], so now, not only [with the

---

[4]*Ibid.*, p. 318.
[5]*Ibid.*, pp. 317,318.

enthusiasm you would show] in my presence but much more because I am absent, work out (cultivate, carry out to the goal, and fully complete) your own salvation with reverence and awe and trembling (self-distrust, with serious caution, tenderness of conscience, watchfulness against temptation, timidly shrinking from whatever might offend God and discredit the name of Christ).

Philippians 2:12

In *The Amplified Bible* this verse is rather long and complicated, but its basic message is set forth clearly and simply in the last part of the *King James Version*: **...work out your own salvation with fear and trembling.**

Since Jesus is the Seed spoken of in Galatians 3:16, when He came to live in us in the form of the Holy Spirit given to us by God the Father, we received a seed of holiness. When Paul tells us to work out our own salvation with fear and trembling, he means that we are to cooperate fully with God by cultivating that seed of holiness that has been sown in us.

The seed of holiness has to be watered with the Word of God. (1 Cor. 3:6.) We all know that as a seed is watered it begins to grow. As we water the seed of holiness in us with the water of the Word (Eph. 5:26.), it begins to grow within us and to spread its branches to every part of our being. Eventually it reaches our mind and affects our thought life. It reaches our heart and affects our mouth, for it is out of the abundance of the heart that the mouth speaks. (Matt. 12:34 KJV.) It reaches our body and affects our facial expressions, our actions, our behavior toward other people. It becomes like a tree or a vine that grows so profusely that it fills up every part of our total being so that there is no place left in us for anything other than the holiness of God.

That is also what is meant by the *process* of sanctification or *growing* in the grace and knowledge of our Lord Jesus

Christ, becoming like Him in every way. (2 Pet. 3:18.) Don't become discouraged if you have not arrived at your destination — if you have not reached your goal. Keep pressing on even if you progress only inch by inch — it is still progress. You are still in the process, and so is everyone else.

Sanctification Is a Work

[Not in your own strength] for it is God Who is all the while effectually at work in you [energizing and creating in you the power and desire], both to will and to work for His good pleasure and satisfaction and delight.

Philippians 2:13

How is this process of sanctification carried out? How is the growth in grace accomplished? Not in our own strength, but by the power of the Holy Spirit Who is at work within us to create in us both the will and the ability to do what pleases the Father.

Do you realize that all the time you have been reading this book, the Holy Spirit has been at work in you, bringing about a change in you, causing you to choose to do the will of God? The Lord did not read this book for you — that was your part — but He did work within you to cause you to want to read it — that is His part.

So here is how the process of sanctification works. You and I receive the gift of God's Holy Spirit Who comes to take up residence within us. Then as we submit ourselves to Him, He works within us, causing us to want to do the will of God, and providing us the strength and power to do that will.

So rather than saying that we are working to please God, it is more accurate to say that God is working in us to make us want to do that which is pleasing to Him. As we yield ourselves and cooperate with Him, we become more and more holy, more and more sanctified in our practical experience.

The Word and the Spirit

So get rid of all uncleanness and the rampant outgrowth of wickedness, and in a humble (gentle, modest) spirit receive and welcome the Word which implanted and rooted [in your hearts] contains the power to save your souls.

But be doers of the Word [obey the message], and not merely listeners to it, betraying yourselves [into deception by reasoning contrary to the Truth].

James 1:21,22

Sanctification is holiness worked out. We become sanctified as all the steps to holiness are taken, as the full process is completed. The Holy Spirit is one agent of that process of sanctification, but there is another agent: the Word.

What it amounts to is this: you and I hear the Word of God, and then the Spirit of God takes that Word and works it in us. It is not our job to work the Word. It is our job to hear the Word and be doers of the Word — by the power of the Spirit Who is at work within us. But it is not us, but the Spirit, Who causes the Word to work.

For so long now we have been taught, "Hear the Word, hear the Word, hear the Word." We have been hearing the Word until we are stuffed with it. That is wonderful. I thank God for it. Yet despite hearing all that Word, we are still not changing as we should. I believe the reason is because there is a missing part — and that part is the Spirit.

Not only must we hear the Word, we must also be yielded to the Holy Spirit within us Who has been given to us to empower us to be able to do the Word.

Just because we hear the Word of God and make an honest effort to apply it in our life does not mean that we deserve for God to do anything for us. We deserve only to die and go to hell. Because in the eyes of God all our righteousness is like filthy rags compared to His righteousness. (Is. 64:6.)

We need to receive and welcome the Word of God with meekness because it alone has the power to save our souls. We must come to God with an attitude of humility, saying to Him, "Father, I am so grateful for this opportunity to hear Your Word. Take this Word that I am hearing and work it in and through me. Holy Spirit, do Your work of sanctification that I may become all that the Father desires for me to be."

All throughout the day we need to have our mind set on the Holy Spirit. Every opportunity possible, turn your thoughts to the presence and power of the Spirit, praying, "Holy Spirit, help me. Teach me. Instruct me. Empower me. Cleanse me. Sanctify me. I am trusting You totally to keep me because You know that I can't do it on my own. Without You I am nothing, I can do nothing, I deserve nothing. Thank You for abiding in me and doing the work in me and through me, to the glory of God the Father."

Reach out to God in faith and thanksgiving, leaning entirely on Him and relying completely on Him, allowing His Word and Holy Spirit to bring you through the process of sanctification to purity and holiness. That is the only way to reach it, the only way to be truly refined and purified.

The Holy Spirit as Refiner's Fire and Fullers' Soap

Behold, I send My messenger, and he shall prepare the way before Me. And the Lord [the Messiah], Whom

you seek will suddenly come to His temple; the Messenger or Angel of the covenant Whom you desire, behold, He shall come, says the Lord of hosts.

But who can endure the day of His coming? And who can stand when He appears? For He is like a refiner's fire and like fullers' soap.

He will sit as a refiner and purifier of silver, and He will purify the priests, the sons of Levi, and refine them like gold and silver, that they may offer to the Lord offerings in righteousness.

Malachi 3:1-3

Here we read an Old Testament prophecy about Jesus, the Messiah, being like a refiner's fire and fullers' soap. Later, in the New Testament we read about the Holy Spirit being like fire. John the Baptist told the people of his day, "I baptize you with water, but there is coming One after me Who will baptize you with the Holy Ghost and with fire." (Matt. 3:11.)

We have heard a lot about the Holy Spirit being like fire, but we have never heard much about His being like fullers' soap.

The Spirit and the Word: The Soap and the Water

However, I am telling you nothing but the truth when I say it is profitable (good, expedient, advantageous) for you that I go away. Because if I do not go away, the Comforter (Counselor, Helper, Advocate, Intercessor, Strengthener, Standby) will not come to you [into close fellowship with you]; but if I go away, I will send Him to you [to be in close fellowship with you].

And when He comes, He will convict and convince the world and bring demonstration to it about sin and about righteousness (uprightness of heart and right standing with God) and about judgment.

John 16:7,8

In this passage Jesus speaks to His disciples about the various roles and functions of the Holy Spirit, one of which is to bring conviction of sin, righteousness and judgment. Then later on in John 17:17-19 Jesus prayed to His Father for His disciples:

> Sanctify them [purify, consecrate, separate them for Yourself, make them holy] by Truth; Your Word is Truth.
>
> Just as You sent Me into the world, I also have sent them into the world.
>
> And so for their sake and on their behalf I sanctify (dedicate, consecrate) Myself, that they also may be sanctified (dedicated, consecrated, made holy) in the Truth.

We have seen how the Holy Spirit works in us, revealing Truth to us, convicting us of sin and righteousness and judgment, and taking the Word and working it in and through us. Now we begin to see Him in another light, as the One Who refines, purifies and sanctifies us by cleansing us of our sins.

In Ephesians 5:25-27 we read these words from the Apostle Paul to the Church:

> Husbands, love your wives, as Christ loved the church and gave Himself up for her.
>
> So that He might sanctify her, having cleansed her by the washing of water with the Word.
>
> That He might present the church to Himself in glorious splendor, without spot or wrinkle or any such things [that she might be holy and faultless].

If you and I could look at ourselves through a spiritual X-ray, we would see a glorious light shining in and through us. But do you know what else we would see deep within? We would see a lot of little black spots. These represent the stains that have been left in our souls by sin.

What can be done to remove these stains so that we can be totally clean and spotless?

What do we do when we get spots on our clothes? We use soap and water. In these passages, we have seen that the Holy Spirit is like fullers' soap, and the Word of God is like water. We have learned that we are sanctified by the Spirit and the Word, by the application of soap and water.

When Dave and I go out to eat, I love to order spaghetti, but it seems that every time I eat it I get it all over my clothes. I used to grab a napkin and start rubbing, trying to get the stain out immediately. Then someone told me that when I did that, I was just grinding it in and making it harder to remove. She told me to leave it alone, adding, "If you'll just wait till you get home, you can take regular bar soap and cold water, and those stains will come right out." But because I am the type who likes to take care of everything right away, it's always hard for me to wait and do it right.

That is the way you and I are in regard to the things of God. We try to remove the spots of sin on our souls by relying on our own efforts instead of being patient and allowing the Lord to remove them by soap and water — by His Spirit and His Word.

But what do we do if the stains are so set in that one application of soap and water doesn't seem to be enough? We apply more soap and let it soak overnight. We have said that soap represents the Holy Spirit, the Spirit of grace, which we defined as the power of God coming into our life to accomplish in us what we cannot accomplish for ourselves by our own effort.

How do we remove stubborn stains left by sin? We apply grace, grace and more grace. Not more scrubbing, not more effort, but more power is what is needed. If one application of God's grace is not enough, then we need to apply more, giving it time to work thoroughly into the stain, saturating it completely. Then when the water of the Word is applied, the stain will be loosened enough that it will come right out.

You and I have available to us the soap of the Spirit and the water of the Word. With them we should be able to witness the clean-up of all the messes in our life.

Grace for All Our Sin

And after you have suffered a little while, the God of all grace [Who imparts all blessing and favor], Who has called you to His [own] eternal glory in Christ Jesus, will Himself complete and make you what you ought to be, establish and ground you securely, and strengthen, and settle you.

To Him be the dominion (power, authority, rule) forever and ever. Amen (so be it).

1 Peter 5:10,11

What should be our response to sin?

As Christians, you and I love God, so we don't want to sin. But it seems that no matter how hard we try not to, eventually we end up falling short of the glory of God. (Rom. 3:23 KJV.) What kind of process do you go through to find peace with God and yourself once you have sinned?

Most of the time the reason I sin is because I don't wait upon the Lord, but try to handle everything for myself. Instead of being patient and allowing the God of grace to work things out for the best, I rush in and try to settle matters on my own. The result is almost always disastrous.

The Holy Spirit has been dealing with me about my habit of jumping to conclusions and judging matters before time. One thing I am particularly bad about is drawing an opinion of other people or their actions or motives without waiting for the Lord to reveal to me what the truth really is.

I also have a tendency to talk too much, to express my opinions too quickly. So it is not surprising that my mouth often gets me into trouble. I say something I shouldn't have said and get someone else angry at me. Even then, instead of allowing the Lord to handle the situation, I work myself into a frenzy trying to remove the spots and stains on the relationship that I myself have caused by my impatience and impulsiveness.

When I sin, instead of applying a generous amount of God's powerful grace, I usually try sprinkling a little dab of guilt and remorse and condemnation on the problem. Rather than confessing my sins to the Lord and receiving His forgiveness right away, I think I have to "suffer for a while." I go around worrying and feeling bad, trying to set the situation right and promising the Lord that if He will just help me get through this mess I will never make that mistake again.

I have done that so much that at least one good thing has come out of it: I have received a lot of revelation about grace!

So after I have messed things up all the way around, what I do — finally — is to stop and say, "Lord, this is not getting me anywhere. Feeling guilty and sorry won't change what has happened. Making resolutions and promises won't keep me from doing the same thing all over again. Working myself into frustration won't set this whole thing right. I surrender myself and this situation to You and ask for Your grace and mercy to keep me in Your perfect peace and to empower me to walk in Your will and way."

In essence, I repent. I open up the channel of faith and ask the Lord to pour grace through that channel. I ask Him to guard me from the sin of presumption, to keep me from jumping to conclusions and judging things and people before I have all the facts.

The Word of God tells us that we receive the promises of God through faith and patience. (Heb. 6:12 KJV.) It assures us that if we will wait upon the Lord, trusting ourselves totally to Him, He Himself will complete us and make us what we ought to be, that He will establish and ground us securely and will strengthen and settle us.

Why must we suffer at all? I believe that many times suffering comes because we have not yet learned to trust God enough to keep us from sinning. Then once we do fall into sin, we are miserable because we feel that we have once again failed ourselves and Him. We hate what we have done and the fact that we don't have the ability to keep ourselves from doing it.

The answer to sin is grace. (Rom. 5:20.) Whatever the cause of our sin and suffering, if we will just keep the channel of faith open we can continue to receive God's solution to all our needs — grace, grace and more grace.

When I see my wrongdoing but cannot change myself, I experience a type of suffering until God delivers me. It actually is a positive thing because when His deliverance comes (and it always does), I rejoice in the grace of God.

The struggling of fleshly effort won't deliver anyone, but God's grace never fails us. If you have big problems, remember that His grace is always sufficient to meet every weakness. (2 Cor. 12:9.)

God does not just offer us grace, but He offers us grace, grace and more grace. His supply is bountiful; no matter how much we use, there is always plenty more.

I encourage you to enter a new realm in your walk with God. Live in His grace and not your own works. The results will be astounding!

Conclusion

The message on grace has been the single most important message that the Holy Spirit has ministered to me. My entire Christian experience was a struggle before I learned about grace. To teach people faith and not teach them grace is, in my opinion, to leave out an important link. I sometimes refer to grace as "the missing link" in the faith walk.

Grace is the power of the Holy Spirit that is available to do what needs to be done in our lives, the power to change what needs to be changed. It is the ability of God which comes to us free for the asking. Grace is so glorious that I could go on and on about all of its wonderful characteristics.

I pray that you will read this book several times over the years. Those of us who are addicted to our own works and efforts usually need several applications of the message on grace to bring healing in our approach to life.

Remember, the grace of God is the exact opposite of works of the flesh. To live by grace may require a change in your approach to almost everything. Don't be discouraged; it will take time.

Always remember that when you feel frustrated it is because you have entered into your own effort and need to get back into God's grace. Grace leaves you strong and calm; works render you weak and powerless, frustrated and frantic.

Through faith the grace of God is received. Faith is not the price that buys the blessings of God, but it is the hand that receives them.

Just hearing the word *grace* is soothing to me. The grace of God makes easy the task that would have been hard or even impossible. Jesus said that His burden is light and easy to be borne. It is the devil who wants to place heavy burdens upon our shoulders — the burden of works of the flesh, the burden of the law and fleshly effort to keep it. But Jesus has promised us that if we will come to Him, He will give us rest. (Matt. 11:28-30).

Don't be satisfied with just enough grace to save you from eternal damnation. Receive not only that grace which saves, but receive grace, grace and more grace so you may live victoriously and glorify Jesus in your daily life.

About the Author

Joyce Meyer has been teaching the Word of God since 1976 and in full-time ministry since 1980. Previously the associate pastor at Life Christian Center in St. Louis, Missouri, she developed, coordinated, and taught a weekly meeting known as "Life In The Word." After more than five years, the Lord brought it to a conclusion, directing her to establish her own ministry and call it *"Life In The Word, Inc."*

Now, her *Life In The Word* radio and television broadcasts are seen and heard by millions across the United States and throughout the world. Joyce's teaching tapes are enjoyed internationally, and she travels extensively conducting *Life In The Word* conferences.

Joyce and her husband, Dave, the business administrator at *Life In The Word,* have been married for over 34 years. They reside in St. Louis, Missouri, and are the parents of four children. All four children are married and, along with their spouses, work with Dave and Joyce in the ministry.

Believing the call on her life is to establish believers in God's Word, Joyce says, "Jesus died to set the captives free, and far too many Christians have little or no victory in their daily lives." Finding herself in the same situation many years ago and having found freedom to live in victory through applying God's Word, Joyce goes equipped to set captives free and to exchange ashes for beauty. She believes that every person who walks in victory leads many others into victory. Her life is transparent, and her teachings are practical and can be applied in everyday life.

Joyce has taught on emotional healing and related subjects in meetings all over the country, helping multiplied thousands. She has recorded more than 210 different audiocassette albums and over 50 videos. She has also authored 39 books to help the body of Christ on various topics.

Her "Emotional Healing Package" contains over 23 hours of teaching on the subject. Albums included in this package are: "Confidence"; "Beauty for Ashes" (includes a syllabus); "Managing Your Emotions"; "Bitterness, Resentment, and Unforgiveness"; "Root of Rejection"; and a 90-minute Scripture/music tape entitled "Healing the Brokenhearted."

Joyce's "Mind Package" features five different audio tape series on the subject of the mind. They include: "Mental Strongholds and Mindsets"; "Wilderness Mentality"; "The Mind of the Flesh"; "The Wandering, Wondering Mind"; and "Mind, Mouth, Moods, and Attitudes." The package also contains Joyce's powerful book, *Battlefield of the Mind*. On the subject of love she has three tape series entitled, "Love Is..."; "Love: The Ultimate Power"; and "Loving God, Loving Yourself, and Loving Others," and a book entitled, *Reduce Me to Love*.

Write to Joyce Meyer's office for a resource catalog and further information on how to obtain the tapes you need to bring total healing to your life.

To contact the author write:

Joyce Meyer Ministries
P. O. Box 655
Fenton, Missouri 63026
or call: (636) 349-0303

Internet Address:
www.jmministries.org

Please include your testimony or help received from this book when you write. Your prayer requests are welcome.

To contact the author
in Canada, please write:

Joyce Meyer Ministries Canada, Inc.
Lambeth Box 1300
London, ON N6P 1T5
or call: (636) 349-0303

In Australia, please write:

Joyce Meyer Ministries-Australia
Locked Bag 77
Mansfield Delivery Centre
Queensland 4122
or call: (07) 3349 1200

In England, please write:

Joyce Meyer Ministries
P. O. Box 1549
Windsor
SL4 1GT
Or call: 01753 831102

Books by Joyce Meyer

A Leader in the Making

"Good Morning, This Is God!" Gift Book

JESUS — Name Above All Names

"Good Morning, This Is God!" Daily Calendar

Help Me — I'm Married!

Reduce Me to Love

Be Healed in Jesus' Name

How to Succeed at Being Yourself

Eat and Stay Thin

Weary Warriors, Fainting Saints

Life in the Word Journal

Life in the Word Devotional

Be Anxious for Nothing —
The Art of Casting Your Cares
and Resting in God

The Help Me! Series:
I'm Alone!
I'm Stressed! • I'm Insecure!
I'm Discouraged! • I'm Depressed!
I'm Worried! • I'm Afraid!

Don't Dread —
Overcoming the Spirit of Dread
with the Supernatural Power of God

Managing Your Emotions
Instead of Your Emotions Managing You

Healing the Brokenhearted

"Me and My Big Mouth!"

NEW: *"Me and My Big Mouth!" Study Guide*